On the outside looking in

On the outside looking in

Collected Essays on Young Child Observation in Social Work Training

Edited by Gillian Bridge
and Gillian Miles

About the Authors

GILLIAN BRIDGE is currently course director of the LSE and Partner's MSc/DipSW Course. She was among the first group of students to undertake the course in child observation sponsored by CCETSW at the Tavistock Institute. Over many years she has been committed to the improvement in quality and quantity of practice learning opportunities. She is an Independent Person under the Children Act for two London boroughs. Her current research interests include children with disabilities in the UK, Jamaica and Eastern Europe.

GILLIAN MILES is a senior clinical lecturer at the Tavistock Clinic where she teaches social work, besides continuing to practice in the multi-disciplinary setting of the Child and Family Department. She has a background of practice in the field of child and family mental health.

Convinced of the importance of observation skills in practice, she has considerable experience of teaching young child observation on post qualification social work courses at the Tavistock Clinic. For the past six years she has organized and been centrally involved in the CCETSW-sponsored course in young child observation for social work tutors and practice teachers, set up to train trainers and so promote good observation teaching both in social work training and other settings.

Published by:
Central Council for Education and Training in Social Work
Derbyshire House, St Chad's Street,
London WC1H 8AD

First published September 1996

Appendix pp. 123–132 © Carfax Publishing Company

ISBN 1 85719 121 8

Designed and typeset by James Shurmer

Printed in England by Latimer Trend

The views expressed in this publication are the authors' and do not necessarily reflect those of CCETSW.

CCETSW is a registered charity.

Cover illustration
Ben Nicholson, *Abstract Box* 1933
Paint and Pencil on Cardboard Box
9.0 × 12.0 cm
Kettle's Yard, University of Cambridge
© Angela Verran-Taunt 1996.

Contents

Foreword   *page* 7

Authors' Acknowledgements   8

Introduction   9

Part I The observer role   13

  1 *Charlene: A child on the outside looking in*   15

  2 *Joe: Some observations on entering the role of observer*   20

Part II The context of observation   27

  3 *Paul: At a university nursery*   29

  4 *Jenny: Blaming the victim, a two year old's experience*   38
    of an institution's defence against anxiety

  5 *Sophie: Managing an adult agenda in a middle*   45
    class family

Part III The cultural context: observing difference   55

  6 *Thomas: A journey into a different territory*   57

  7 *Bina: Observing cultural difference*   66

Part IV Attachments and separations: normal life events   71

  8 *Ben: Depression or developmental delay?*   73

  9 *Anthony: Responding to a mother's return to work*   80

10 *David: The birth of his brother*   88

Part V Getting into deep waters   93

11 *Kerrie: A view of an infant survivor*   95

12 *Sam and James: Can you hear me mother?*   103

Part VI Application of learning from observation for   111
social workers, practice teachers and tutors

13 *George: Transferred learning from child*   113
    observation to social work and practice teaching

Postscript: Some ways forward   121

Appendix: Trowell, J. and Miles, G.   123
'The contribution of observation training to professional
development in social work'
reprinted from Journal of Social Work Practice Vol. 5 No. 1, 1991
with permission

References and further reading   133

Foreword

There is growing evidence from child abuse enquiry reports that professionals often fail to focus on the child's perspective. One way to avoid losing this perspective is to include child observation in social work training at the professional and post professional levels. In adopting the role of "observer", the student will often struggle to stay with the child's experience, and see at times "what adult carers did not see or allow themselves to see" (Trowell and Miles 1991).

The essays in this book were written to promote the use of child observation in social work training by social work tutors and practice teachers who took part in CCETSW-funded training in child observation, organized in a variety of different locations by the Tavistock Clinic between 1989 and 1995. The trainers were trained to take their learning and experience into their colleges and agencies.

Towards the end of the training each member of the programme wrote an essay about a theme central to their experience. Through the observer's eye the reader will inevitably feel the powerful impact of what was sometimes a child's painful experience. While observation training has long been used as part of psychotherapy training, this marks the first material to be published by and for the social work profession.

The essay writers chose their own focus. They wrote from their own experience, and the interpretations in individual papers are also their own.

Our hope is that the publication of this group of essays will promote a wider interest in, and a greater understanding of, the value of observational learning which has already started in some training programmes. Over 100 tutors and practice teachers from across the UK have completed the three-term part-time training, and many are developing observation training as part of their own training programmes. A number of DipSW programmes now incorporate sessions of child observation and linked seminars. Some of those trained are developing training in agencies, and including staff from other disciplines.

The CCETSW funding for this project has come to an end, but the Tavistock Clinic is committed to offering both further training where there is demand, and consultation to tutors and practice teachers who are training others.

The authors' vivid accounts in these essays of personal experiences are accessible to tutors, practice teachers and students alike as an introduction to the complex skill of observation. They complement *Keeping Children in Mind: Training Manual and Video on Child Observation* (Ellis *et al.* 1996), written by former students of the course and published, with accompanying video, as a companion volume.

To protect the anonymity of the children, their families and carers, names and locations and some family details have been changed and we have decided not to name the individual authors. For this reason we are all the more grateful for their permission to publish their accounts of their very personal experience. Gillian Bridge and Gillian Miles have edited the essays in ways that have skilfully grouped them into themes and given them some cohesiveness without losing their freshness. We owe them considerable gratitude for their work and commitment.

We also wish to thank the *Journal of Social Work Practice* for permission to include as an appendix the paper on the contribution of observation training to social work by Judith Trowell and Gillian Miles, which will give readers a more detailed appreciation of the teaching of observation skills and their place in social work training.

Clare Roskill (former CCETSW Child Care Projects Manager)
July 1996

Authors' Acknowledgements

Our thanks go first to the children, their families and carers who agreed to take part in these observations. To protect the confidentiality of these participants, the authors of the essays, unfortunately, cannot be named and we are therefore the more grateful to them. Members of the seminar groups, and the skilled seminar leaders also deserve our thanks. Without them the course could not have been held.

We are particularly grateful to Judith Trowell and Elizabeth Oliver Bellasis who, as the first seminar leaders, have both continued to contribute a very great deal in many ways to the project throughout; Judith also suggested the Ben Nicholson painting used on the cover.

Thanks are also due to the Children Services (SSI) Section of the Department of Health Social Care Group who made it possible for CCETSW to fund the project and to the CCETSW staff involved. Peter Fry originated the idea for the project, Claire Roskill, was its project manager, Ed Pritchard, Publications Manager, and George Smith, Editorial Adviser, edited the copy and managed its printing.

Finally our thanks go to Geraldine Drew for her infinite patience in coping with the many necessary redraftings.

Gillian Bridge, Gillian Miles
July 1996

Introduction

This book is designed to acquaint social work tutors, practice teachers and their students with the experience of observing young children. Presented in the form of a collection of essays describing observational experience, the material is vivid, and speaks for itself, with little need for introduction. Each essay may be read separately, but as a whole they convey the wealth of learning that can be gained from observational studies.

The essays were written by tutors and practice teachers on a CCETSW-sponsored course, designed to promote the use of observation training as part of social work training. CCETSW sponsored the training to ensure that there would be a group of skilled trainers, who could go on to teach in necessarily modified ways on their own programmes. The intention was to give social work tutors and practice teachers experience of being an observer, so that they could think about teaching observation before preparing others to observe. Each member of the course was asked to find a child, at home or in a day care setting, and arrange to observe them every week for a year, attending weekly seminars during that time to think about the observations. An account of the method and of the first year of the course by Trowell and Miles is reprinted in the appendix.

Use of observation in psychotherapy training is well established and a range of literature, such as *Closely Observed Infants* edited by L. M. Miller, (1989) and *Backwards in Time* by A. Piontelli (1986) written from a psychotherapy perspective is available. The essays do not replicate this work but demonstrate the importance of observation in social work training which, while drawing on the same central learning core, has different emphases. Based on small group seminars and with an emphasis on learning through experience, our style of learning has been similar to that for psychotherapists.Recognition of the importance of observation skills in social work training came out of collaboration between three people – Peter Fry at CCETSW, Marilyn Pietroni, then a Senior Clinical Lecturer in Social Work at the Tavistock Clinic, and Judith Trowell, Child Psychiatrist at the Tavistock Clinic. All three were involved in the working group that produced *Right or Privilege* (ed. Pietroni, M., CCETSW 1991) on post qualification training in child care social work, which emphasized the importance of observational skills. While some social work programmes already include observation training, for it to be taught well, trainers need to be trained.

The course, which started with an intake of 10 tutors from across England and Wales coming to two seminar groups at the Tavistock Clinic in London, has run for over five years. During that time, locally-based seminar groups from across England and Wales were set up which met together as a whole course group three times a year for study days, providing opportunities for some of the theoretical aspects of the teaching to be addressed. About 100 social work trainers across the UK have completed the training, and many have gone on enthusiastically to introduce observation to their training programmes. Time constraints have meant that DipSW students usually undertake observations over a more limited period.

People with good knowledge of child development and background theories and first hand experience of observation have led seminars. As described in Appendix 1, the seminar leaders on this course have taught from a range of theoretical perspectives – attachment theory and child development; a systemic framework; a psychodynamic framework; and culture, class, race and gender.

Their central task, however, has been to support tutors and practice teachers in finding and maintaining their observer role, and to provide a base to which those on the course can bring their experiences, however difficult, for discussion. Seminars, thus facilitated, provide the space for both personal, experiential and intellectual learning and, within this basic framework, a wide range of different learning perspectives can be addressed.

Selecting the essays

This book was born out of the growing pile of unseen papers arising from the course which spoke graphically about the value of observation. The particular essays chosen seemed to us to convey between them many of the important themes and possibilities of observational learning. Each essay has its own personal style which we have retained. They also differ in approach – some are mainly the account of the child as seen in the observation setting, others include more of what it felt like to be an observer; some include references to the literature, others stay with the narrative account.

They are grouped under headings linking central themes which emerged for us during selection. We have taken as section headings the observer role, the setting, culture and class differences, attachments and separations in ordinary life experience, and the personal and professional learning that comes from observation. A section is included on "difficult observations", those which did not work out exactly as expected, but provided rich, albeit painful, learning experience. Yet, to some extent, our groupings are arbitrary, merely underlining the writers' central preoccupations.

The importance of discriminatory and cultural issues is acknowledged and inequalities and differences in society permeate the essay collection. However, although there is a section focusing on cultural difference, the reader's attention is also drawn at various points to the wider debates about discrimination and ethnicity.

Some authors have set their experiences in a theoretical context to give them meaning. Thus, there are passages on Bion's theory of containment, on the contribution of Isobel Menzies Lyth to the understanding of institutional defences against anxiety, and on John Bowlby's contribution to the understanding of attachments. These provide the context and are central to the essays. However, we have not attempted to address the wide theoretical background of all the subject areas which can be touched on through observations though this is further discussed in the Appendix. A short bibliography has been provided for those interested in reading further.

Because of the painful everyday experiences described, descriptions of some of the situations of the children observed may be difficult to read. Through as it were setting a microscope on the action, the observation process draws attention to some painful issues we might otherwise have overlooked such as the effects of attachments and separations, or missing the child's cues, or the normal process of the birth of a sibling. One writer quotes George Eliot's *Middlemarch* (1871) "If we had a keen vision and feeling of all ordinary human life, it would be like hearing the grass grow and the squirrel's heart beat, and we should die of the roar which lies the other side of silence". Observation removes that filtering process, leaving us open to the pain of everyday experience, but we hope that the extraordinary resilience of both children and their parents comes through.

The other side of the coin is the observer's heightened awareness of self, stripped of the professional role and activity. Without doubt, this has been a major part of the learning process, and one that has made a lasting impression on many course members. "As well as being an observer observing a family, I was provided with further opportunity in the seminars to reflect about the observational process, both about what was recorded of what was seen and about the nature of the perceiver. The seminar experience heightened awareness of myself as a participant in the group; as an observer of a child and as an individual. Increased self-awareness is not always a comfortable process, but the group was a reasonably safe place to explore boundaries"

Applications to social work learning

Child observation emerges through the book as a skill with a wide range of applications in professional training, and as a rich learning opportunity. The associated learning can be powerful, often in unexpected ways. There are examples in these essays of emerging questions, for example, about the role of women in our society, and in different cultures; about childrens' awareness of difference; about cultural expectations of children. Questions are raised around our assumptions about day-care provision for young children, and the painful adjustments that have to be made in the ordinary transitions of life – for the child from home to nursery, or, for the parent returning to work, from closeness to more separateness. Central, of course, is the observer's experience of rich personal learning.

Uses of the book

The essays are intended primarily for professional readers, both those who teach observation on social work programmes either in colleges or within practice agencies, and students who may be setting out to do their own observations. It is primarily a book about observation, designed to convey its learning potential in the field of child care, and social work training. Used in this way, individual essays may contribute to preparation for the observation role, as a group of students prepare to set up their own observations. Here the focus would be on aspects of the essays which highlighted the role of the observer and the personal impact of observation.

Other potential for learning from individual essays include bringing to life the organizational aspects of day care, day nurseries, child-minding, fostering or alternative day care; theoretical perspectives, such as child development or attachment theory; aspects of difference – race, class and culture – and personal learning which crosses all the essays. As is evident in the final essay on application of learning, observation has particular relevance to practice teaching. It provides learning about the place of observation skills in the professional role, their value in assessment and the need for assessment over time.

However, mindful of the painfulness of some of the observations, we would emphasize the need for seminar discussion alongside any reading, just as we emphasize the importance of the supporting seminar for any observation learning (see Appendix for further discussion). As the writers of the essays point out time and again, it is the actual experience of being an observer which carries the greatest potential for learning.

We would refer all those setting out on teaching child observation to the complementary manual of observation training in social work with associated video by Lynda Ellis, Ivis Lasson, and Robin Solomon (1996).

In many ways, observation is a hard personalized learning tool, but very effective. We hope that these essays bring its potential to life.

Part I
The Observer Role

1 Charlene: A child on the outside looking in   15

2 Joe: Some observations on entering the role   20
   of observer

Introduction

The common link between essays in this book is the process of negotiating, establishing, sustaining and learning from and about the observer role. It usually provokes powerful feelings of uncertainty and anxiety in students as they perceive young children's lives with greater intensity and more detail than usual, leading to requests for firm definitions and boundaries. As one course participant said "we need more signposts along the way!".

The two essays selected for this part about Charlene and Joe may not provide the requested signposts, but reveal child observation to be a dynamic process; evolving in time; constantly presenting dilemmas about the nature of the role, and providing skills training in maintaining boundaries. They all illustrate how being too prescriptive about definitions of role may be less helpful than regular reviews of an evolving process through recording and seminar discussion.

These essays show the child observation role to be challenging and creative and relevant to those training to work with children.

1 Charlene: A child on the outside looking in

In this young child observation I viewed a plethora of dynamics and emotional events between a group of children, their carers and their parents. Following each observation, in recording the nature of these interactions and discussing them in the seminar group, I began to see that interaction between those that I was observing had implications for:

- the child in terms of the development and fulfilment of needs;

- group carers of children and the impact this has on individual children;

- all aspects of assessing children;

- me as an observer - individually and professionally.

Setting

I chose a playgroup local to my place of social work employment. This playgroup was in the heart of a very busy Christian community centre in a large hall beneath a church. There were two full-time staff who were church members in charge of the group. The remaining three staff were non church members and worked part-time. All staff were white women who held the Pre-School Playgroup Association Foundation Course qualification.

Each day is structured as follows:

9.45–11.00 a.m. Free play which included creative activities, table top toys, home corner, sand and water.

11.00–11.15 a.m. Snack and drink.

11.15–11.45 a.m. Physical play, bikes and outdoor activities.

11.45–12.00 noon. Story time and singing

Parents were encouraged to stay with their children until staff thought they had settled and to spend one morning per term helping with the staff.

Charlene: the observed child

Charlene is a three-year-old black, female child of African-Caribbean descent. My introduction to Charlene and her father was through the staff at the playgroup who helped me with the task of negotiating my observation with her father.

Charlene is the youngest of three children. She has a nine-year-old brother and an eight-year-old sister, who both attend schools locally. Charlene was brought into the playgroup by her father on Mondays, Wednesdays and Thursdays. She spends Tuesdays at home with her mother, who does not work on that particular day. When not at the playgroup Charlene's primary carer is her father.

My selection of Charlene from a group of 32 children was informed by my wish as a black person to observe a black child. A further dynamic was the fact that at the time of selection, Charlene was also the only black child in the playgroup who attended consistently.

Charlene's interaction with the playgroup carers

Observing the relationship between Charlene and her playgroup carers highlighted some thought-provoking issues for me. I noted from the outset that Charlene frequently chose activity tables where there were no playgroup carers with whom she could interact. I thought about this, querying whether Charlene was really the quiet child that the staff kept telling me she was. I then noted that Charlene's distance from the staff was being reciprocated, observing that times when they approached her spontaneously were fairly rare. Subsequently, one common feature of this child-carer interaction was that neither freely approached the other. This made me think about the issue of caregiver-child avoidance and why it existed. However, in trying to define the nature of the playgroup carers' interaction with Charlene, I observed that the carers who were church members interacted differently with Charlene from the carers who were non-church members.

The former group of carers tended to assert their authority over Charlene, whether their commands were justified or not. Their interactions also tended to be dominant and directive. These staff members rarely played with Charlene, preferring to lead her around the room.

During my second observation, I noted that Jenny, one such staff member, approached Charlene at the painting table. Charlene was not painting as she could find no paper. She stood next to a painting completed by another child. Jenny went over to Charlene, wrote her name on the picture saying "Well done", and walked off. Charlene had not painted this picture and had little time to tell Jenny this before she was gone again. There were frequent similar occurrences in other observations:

Jenny comes over and sees the situation. However, Jenny misinterprets the group of three girls standing at the table and interprets it as Charlene and the other girl fighting for a seat ... Jenny then sits Charlene down in a seat ... gathers up Charlene's 'playdoh'* from the other table, ... Charlene seemed confused.

Hence, this dominant and directive interaction imposed upon Charlene also meant that these members of staff were failing to identify Charlene's needs and circumstances.

The non-church member playgroup carers did not seem to be as directive in their approach to children. They actually engaged in playing with the children. However, they played with a select group of children, whom they approached spontaneously, and were approached in return by these children. Those not selected watched from the periphery and I observed Charlene to be one of them. Examples of this could be seen in an observation where Charlene followed her friend Jane over to a staffed activity table.

* Playdoh is a commercial name for a kind of plasticine used by young children.

Once there, Charlene stood and watched while staff played with her friend and cuddled her. Charlene followed Jane to the activity table. There Jane got a lot of attention and cuddles. The staff joked with her and did jigsaw puzzles with her while she sat on their lap.

Charlene stood at the side of the table, desperately trying to get Jane's attention. She played alone with a jigsaw until Jane got off Rose's lap. Rose did not offer Charlene a place at the table, neither did she acknowledge Charlene's presence.

Subsequently I observed Charlene working quite hard in her attempt to get some attention while with her friend Jane. Further, these playgroup carers seemed only to interact with Charlene when it was absolutely necessary and even then their response to her seemed to be at a diminished pace:

Rose crosses the room to sort out John's attack on Charlene ... when she gets there, the bean bag ... had burst ... Rose diverts her attention to helping John pick up the spilled beans instead of comforting Charlene.

The quality and quantity of interaction between Charlene and her playgroup carers caused me much concern. I questioned its significance in relation to Charlene's race. However, during one observation, the staff gave much attention to another black female child who entered the group on one occasion.

As soon as Mandy, a little black girl, entered the room with her mother almost all staff called out to her. She ran around literally basking in all the attention she was receiving.

I questioned Charlene's age, querying whether the staff communicated better with the older children - given that Charlene was one of the younger children in the group. Finally, I questioned Charlene's gender - having also observed that the more dominant staff engaged well with the boys in more boisterous games of 'spiderman'. Nevertheless, it seemed to me that I observed group care where carers only gave attention to those children who reached out for it. Hence, those children who had more low key attention-seeking behaviour, like Charlene, were not noticed. I was then left questioning the negative impact of the carers' non-interaction on Charlene and these children.

The nature of this interaction led me to think about attachment theory and recent American research (Hennessy, *et al.* 1992) on the role of the caregiver in day care.

Research reported in this study consistently showed that if the carer is more sensitive to a child's needs, the child will be more securely attached to the carer. Hence, I can only conclude that Charlene may have approached her carers more freely if they had been more sensitive to her needs by approaching her, positively interacting with her and not misjudging her needs or situations in which they found her.

Interaction with Charlene as an observer

A second dynamic which arose from my observation was my interaction with Charlene and the significance that this held. Given the size of the hall it was not too difficult to find a space from which to observe Charlene. At the beginning of the

17

observations, I often chose a place across the room from which to observe her. Subsequently, my interaction with Charlene was not so far away, as she did not tend to be concerned by my then distant presence.

I found Bentzen's work (1985) useful in thinking about how Charlene played. She seemed to display 'onlooker behaviour' initially as she spent most of her time watching other children play.

With the continuation of my observation I found that Charlene's play progressed, moving on to 'parallel play' - where she played close to children, but remained independent of them. By the fourth observation, Charlene displayed 'associative play', where she played with particular children, sharing toys, following them around and attempting to control who else played with them.

As Charlene moved from 'onlooker behaviour' through to 'associative play', I felt the need to get closer to her to see in more detail aspects of her development and communication. Interestingly, as I drew closer to Charlene, she continued to ignore my presence. However, it was not Charlene who showed changes in behaviour given my proximity - it was her playgroup carers who reacted. During the fourth observation, a playgroup carer drew close to where Charlene was playing with a little boy:

From some distance away Janet, a playleader, glanced over disapprovingly. Jenny then comes over to where I am sitting near Charlene and Peter ... She kneels down and asks Charlene about her brother and sister. Jenny then stands up ... looks across at me and comments 'She has come out of her shell'. She then walks back to her desk.

The impact of my proximity to Charlene arose again, several observations later, when I sat next to her at a staffed activity table:

... a second later Jenny came back. She took Charlene by the hand and told a worker standing nearby ... very loudly "whenever I see Charlene with her father outside ... school, Charlene ignores her dad and stands with me"

My presence and interaction with Charlene obviously raised issues for Charlene's carers and had implications for this child. As a consequence, Charlene began to get more attention from the staff. Did they find my proximity to Charlene threatening? This made me think about the implications this had for my contact with children and their parents in other settings as a social worker. I began to wonder how parents might change their pattern of interaction with their children given the presence of a social worker. Having seen the impact that my presence had as an observer, I am now very sensitive to the issue of my presence when making social work visits to families and how parents may create an artificial environment while I assess their interaction with their children.

Over and above being a threat to the staff, I experienced difficulty in remaining the observer and not entering the role of a caregiver to Charlene and some of the other children on the periphery. Although Charlene did not approach me, I struggled not to approach her when she was in any difficulty unnoticed by staff.

Conclusion

With my increased awareness of the interaction and dynamics between the child, her carers and then myself as the observer, I tried to make sense of the type of child Charlene was.

Each week I experienced a mix of emotions where I hypothesized and questioned her quietness, her being among, yet on the periphery of the children; her being dominated by certain staff members and ignored by others, and her being the only black child. I came to the conclusion that Charlene was a child on the 'outside looking in'. But each week I visited, she refuted my hypothesis by acting in a manner that I did not anticipate. Looking back I now realize that I was seeking to assess this child by deciding what type of child she was, before I had completed my assessment of her. In making social work assessments of families, it is often all too easy to decide what the outcome will be, before entering a family setting. Hence the significance of the interactions within this playgroup setting became clearer to me as aspects relevant to my own professional practice were highlighted. Being the only black woman in the setting, observing the only black child, I was left thinking about how my presence was a threat to the staff. This is certainly an issue of race but it is inextricably linked to being a social worker, making visits to families and how parents may alter their interaction with their children given the presence of assessors/social workers.

I was aware of going in with the assumption that racism may have been the cause of Charlene's being overlooked. I learnt a great deal from the process of observation as what I saw were many subtle processes which may have included racial issues at work in the day care setting.

I had noticed that a little boy was walking around with his coat on and a plastic bag in his hand. Minutes later Jenny shouted out 'swimming'. This little boy went immediately to the front of the room to Jenny followed by Charlene and Jane and most of the other children to find out what the announcement was about. As Jenny and Janet openly debated which children they would substitute to make up the numbers for the trip, Charlene stood directly in front of them looking up at them. She then went to a nearby activity table. She did not participate. She sat still watching the outcome of Jenny and Janet's search for children. She got up again, resuming her standing position before Jenny and Janet, but moments later Janet had her required number of children and left. Charlene then marched in the opposite direction to the far end of the room.

With hindsight, I also realize that my initial reaction to the treatment of this child was outrage. But I now question how much of this was the fact that I brought my own personal issues to the observations. I became aware of the complexity of factors contributing to the quality of experience for a young child in a playgroup and I became cautious in assessing the dynamic process I witnessed each time. The seminar group was instrumental in helping me to separate out my own issues from those of the quality of child care I saw in the observation setting. During these discussions I began to see the strength of this child and her coping mechanisms, a perception which provided me with the strength and skills to complete the observation process.

2 Joe: Some observations on entering the role of observer

Of the numerous themes that have emerged during my observation, any of which could have constituted an essay in its own right, one that has continuously interested me in its various guises, has been the experience of being an observer in this particular family, and by extension, the role of the observer more generally.

The family I visited were Lloyd and Olga, the parents, and Kevin and Joe, their children. Olga was a woman in her early thirties, of French extraction. She was slender and brown haired. Lloyd, her husband, the father of the children, was also in his thirties, a Londoner, stocky in stature, who was self employed locally. (Although the observer met him when setting up the observation he was not present at any other time.) Joe was four months old when I first met him. He had a mass of light brown hair in big, loose curls, blue eyes and a ready broad smile. Kevin, his brother, was five years old. He also had a mass of thick, curly hair and intense eyes. He was bright and agile for his age.

As a teacher of social work/child care in the 1980s/90s, it is impossible for me not to be conscious of the Department of Health research findings and the recommendations of the numerous local authority enquiries into the deaths of children in care, relating to the relationships, or rather the lack of them, that social workers have with the children for whom they are responsible:

"Throughout the three years of social work with the Beckfords, Ms. Wahlstrom totally mis-conceived her role as the fieldworker enforcing care orders in respect of two very young children at risk. Her gaze focused on Beverley Lorrington and Morris Beckford; she averted her eyes to the children to be aware of them only as and when they were with their parents, hardly even to observe their development, and never to communicate with Jasmine on her own." (L. B. Brent, 1985, p. 293)

Similarly:

"The result was that while Claudette received the lion's share of social work attention, responding to it only passively and evasively, Tyra was largely overlooked". (L. B. Lambeth, 1982, page 165)

Research findings highlight the fact that social workers tend to form relationships with the parents of children for whom they hold statutory responsibility, rather than with the children themselves. The reasons for this seem to be primarily because it is easier, or more common, or more comfortable to form adult-to-adult relationships. What they do not refer to directly, and I have been thinking about these issues more recently, are in fact the deeper, psychological reasons why social workers might not form relationships directly with the children. One has to do with defending against the painful experiences the children are having, and by coming too close we too must experience that pain and so therefore withdraw from the children themselves; the other one seems to relate to situations where the powerful needs of the parents to engage the worker for themselves, and the unconscious processes which get played out or projected onto the worker have the effect of excluding the child. Many of my colleagues' observations have been examples of the former reason for avoidance or engaging directly with the child. In other words, the painful experience of the child evokes anxiety, sadness and depression in the worker, who, were they not to have the support of a seminar group, would have 'missed' many of those experiences, through blocking, avoiding or misunderstanding. Whereas my observation has illustrated the latter: the parent whose dynamics manage seemingly to control and compete for the observer's attention.

At the beginning we struggled in our seminar group to conceptualize the role of the observer and the dilemmas it presented to each of us.

"Much thought has to be given to the central problem of the role of the observer in the whole situation. This problem seemed to be twofold, as it involved the conceptualization of the observer's role and also the conscious and unconscious attitudes of the observer." (Bick 1963, pp.558-9)

Being met therefore with a family where I could not seem to establish a clear observational vantage point, felt very much like my own inadequacy until a theme started to emerge about control. A large aspect of this was about Olga's controlling my position through her need for me to assume various roles at different times. Thus, during the course of the observation I was projected into roles as her 'student', her 'colleague', a 'social worker', her 'friend', her 'possible business partner', her 'substitute partner', and her 'baby sitter'. The sense of being controlled was more basic even than role allocation, which I will return to later in the essay.

On my first visit I was met with an Olga who had decided she was going to the High Road, and therefore I should accompany her. In spite of my attempt to explain that I had anticipated observing in the home, she agreed we could in the future, but then set off. Once outside the shops, I was relegated to stand with the pushchair, which I remember left me with a sense of relief that even if it was on the street I could observe Joe for the first time. Early write-ups were sprinkled with places where I noted that although Olga had given me a choice, I experienced a sensation of not really having a choice. This manifested itself around where I sat, what room I sat in, and when I was given 'permission' to do certain things, which normally felt like I was being told to do them. Impressions following write-ups often contained some reference to feeling controlled;

Again, but not as powerfully as three weeks ago, I had the feeling of Olga having everything (and everybody) very organized and being well in control (in the nicest possible sense). Very unflappable, very competent, (probably very safe and consistent) but a very dominant figure. Not 'imposing' control, but being in control.

It was through the experience of feeling controlled that I began to recognize the way Olga was controlling with the children as well, and considered whether I was mirroring their experience. Nowhere was this demonstrated more clearly than in Olga's continuing references to Joe being wilful;

(he was nine months) ... he's getting very wilful you know. He really has a mind of his own. Children have different personalities you know, and he's very wilful ... but he really

21

is very cheeky. Already sometimes we're having a clash of wills. Mine is still stronger, but he's very wilful.

Presumably this grew from her feelings that Joe was just like her in personality and temperament (unlike Kevin). But while she never acknowledged, nor seemed aware of her controlling nature, if Joe was just like her, and there was inevitably going to be the 'clash of the titans' then logically she was the other titan.

On the other hand, her control in relation to Kevin took on a completely different form. He had been the obedient and therefore controllable child, until shortly before the beginning of my observations. Olga's perception was that he was getting more and more out of control since he started school (five months into the observation). I experienced Kevin as polite, obedient, and well behaved given he is five years old, but Olga seemed to get more strict, and less patient as the year progressed.

"He gets more rude and cheeky every day, I'm sure he's learning it at school. It's the kids he mixes with, he wasn't like that when he was in here all the time with us."

This moves into a parallel theme about inside/outside – what is inside is controllable and therefore good, but what is outside is bad because it is uncontrollable.

There emerged a clear picture of outside being dangerous, as opposed to safety inside. During the period of time I visited, the brakes of a lorry failed on the hill outside the house and a lady passing by was pushed against the wall.

"You could hear the crash from in here. When I rushed out, her shoe, with her foot in it was in front of the house, her body had been dragged down the road ... she was in her thirties, she'd just gone down the road to get a bottle of milk, her husband didn't even know she had gone out ... he just waited for hours, no one told him, the police didn't know where she lived" ... all of this was said so matter of factly, concerned, horrified even, but unemotional.

A house backing onto the garden caught fire in the night. Two young children died in the blaze: their mother could not rescue them.

"I phoned the fire brigade when I saw the flames, I'm sure many people did ... there were men leaning out of the neighbouring windows yelling for the mother of the children not to go near ... she was screaming, but none of them came down to help" ... I felt horrified by Olga's story, but I had this weird sensation for a moment that she was making it up. I'm sure it was true, but there was something about the tone of her voice that made it unreal.

Another serious road accident happened in front of the house, the wreckage of which remained out there for weeks, but which also had an emotionless quality when she related it to me.

There were a series of local disasters which appeared throughout our conversations; indecent exposures, gang fights, rapes and burglaries.

Her good controlled 'inside' boy was being tainted by 'outside' experiences; thus Kevin's clashes of will with her were not because he was just like her, but because he had become contaminated by the uncontrollable outsiders. In contrast, Joe's were attributed to his likeness to her. Each incident of testing limits, or becoming more independent, became a battle for control – and while Olga imposed her will firmly, more subtle acts of defiance emerged, one of which was to try to engage me as his ally.

Another very powerful dynamic arose in this regard, namely, that Kevin was competing for my attention, to move me out of the observer role into a relationship with him. He looked to me to collude in his subtle resistances; he developed a pattern of leaving me time alone with Joe and Olga, but each week, just as it was time for me to go, to get me to stay and spend time with him by 'just for a few minutes, read me a story' or 'just play this new game one time before you go' or arrive to tell me something that happened to him that day.

At least once in most observations, he would suddenly rush in or rush up and kiss, cuddle or tickle Joe, in what each time I perceived as an aggressive way. When Olga saw it she always commented on how much Kevin loves Joe; but Kevin responded to my observer role and appeared to know that I'd 'observed' something different.

At that Kevin rushed over to him, threw himself onto his knees so as to be on a level with Joe and began hugging and kissing him wildly and making loud smacking noises ... Letting him go, he said to me, at first garbled so I wasn't sure I'd heard it right, "I don't hate him, I love him, I love Joe", and then repeating it, "I don't hate him, I LOVE him", much more loudly, by now climbing back onto the sofa next to me and smiling. Olga came back at that point and sat on the armchair and Joe crawled over to her and started to cry.

Olga always termed these interactions love, and praised Kevin for how good he was with his little brother, but in my role as observer, without commenting, I gave Kevin the opportunity to say how he really felt and be heard without risk. The experience of sharing it, however, moved the focus of my observation more directly onto Kevin, and away from Joe who was meant to be the target of my attention.

In an attempt to understand this shift in focus that was becoming more difficult to disengage from as time progressed, I realized that one further theme in this family, was about where feelings reside. Without doubt, Kevin was the holder of feelings for this family. To me, Olga seemed to be in constant motion and I marvelled at the efficiency, the creative activities mode with which she operated with the children. I started to understand this as a possible avoidance of feelings, a perpetual motion that left no room for sadness or bad feelings. Olga discussed in the same matter of fact tones, disasters, personal problems, and recipes. In fact, more than matter of fact, there was a strong need to joke about, or make light of the very things that were painful. Thus her relationship with Joe, which was caring, loving and competent, was also about avoiding his pain and making him laugh. Joe, the focus of my observation, was an infant who smiled, and laughed easily. This was the part of herself that she saw reflected in him.

Comments she made about the boys kept echoing:

"He's just like me this one" (Joe). "He has mad moments" ... (to him) "you're just like your mummy" ... (to me) "Kevin wasn't like that. He was a quite sensible child. He was grown up from the time he was born".

Sometimes for no reason Kevin just burst into tears, and when I ask him why, he says "I don't know, it's just all these feelings inside".

"You know that old folk song about the old man in the streets of London" (she hums) "Kevin's class learned it in school: he sang it to me, and he was crying. 'It's so sad mummy', he said, 'can you imagine'" ... and she laughed.

I set out in this paper to explore the role of the observer, and having presented the above themes would like to suggest that it was only through analysing what was so difficult about remaining in the observer role, or more specifically keeping the identified child as the continued focus of my observation, that I could learn the themes and dynamics; in other words, it was by realizing that I was the mirror that I could see their experiences within the family more clearly.

Conclusion

Thus during my first entry into the family as an observer in spite of Olga's welcoming and enthusiasm I remained physically outside where dangers reside, and experienced the full impact of her control. At the time I felt as if I must have done it wrong and had failed at being an observer ... in retrospect, I think, to have imposed what I thought I had to do on her would have necessitated asserting my resistance to her control which would I think have moved me more directly out of the observer role. Over the following weeks, by allowing myself to be controlled, in spite of uneasiness, I was to enter the role of the observer, by experiencing what it felt like for 'the observed'. It took 15 weeks to stop feeling controlled (in fact it never really stopped but I began to feel differently about it later) and to realize that I had been observing, but not what I'd anticipated being able to see.

If I had gone in as the social worker with an 'agenda' I might well have missed an important dynamic and provoked a different response. As an observer I was under no such pressure, and so I could watch and wait. That absolution from doing made the space both to see the observed, as well as to become aware of my own traits and feelings, my own projections and counter transferences. It was the dissonance between what I wanted spontaneously to do but contained, that was the key to my understanding.

I began this paper with the research and inquiry findings about the difficulties social workers face in keeping the child as the focus, and how, instead of seeing the child, they form relationships with the adults. My observation is both an example and an explanation of this phenomenon. Interestingly, I have detailed recordings of 37 visits, large amounts of which focus on Joe and what I observed of him. I think I could have written a number of papers about interesting insights through the help of my seminar group about how his behaviour and responses reflected his inner world. Ironically I have overlooked Joe in the paper I finally produced. What I have reflected is how attention digresses, gets lost or stolen from the child who is the identified focus of that attention, and that there are a lot of things, people and issues competing for that central focus.

Why was it so hard to keep Joe in mind? Partly because the parent, or other participants, in this case Olga and Kevin, engaged me to meet their needs, and because I allowed myself to be controlled. Interestingly some of my most detailed observations about Joe are at the very times I made a conscious effort to resist and focus on him. That often meant having to choose. I can well appreciate why social workers, when working with much more demanding and needy adults than Olga, are unable to withstand being taken over by the parents' needs. The easiest observations were those when she and Joe operated as a unit because then I didn't need to split my attention; by focusing on mum I was of necessity focusing on the child. In those instances where the parent-child dyad does not ever function as a dyad, it could be impossible to see the child unless you consciously imposed that on the person (against probable resistance). Thus the need to reinforce that awareness in social work training is crucial, and perhaps there would be no better way to experience it than to come to it through being an observer. So in considering why I struggled with keeping Joe at the centre of my observation, it is important to look at the competition for the focus of my attention. Thus, I started out by being put into the role of Olga's 'student', that she might teach me all about child development, and thus control me. It took a long time to be moved from there, and I re-emerged projected into that role during particular periods. She attempted to move me into the role of friend, to equalize us, by inviting me to her social activities, at which point I had to resist most actively, and was met I believe with some anger and hurt. I was thrust into a babysitting role once, perhaps as a test, and even experienced myself being projected into father's role when his long working hours kept him away late. She even at one point suggested we became business partners running a nursery, knowing nothing of my practice, but of course not based on reality, but on her needs and transferences.

During those times that Olga and Joe were a dyad, or at the times I was able to observe Joe because she was able to allow him to have my attention, Kevin was another competitor, and he had a very powerful magnet by engaging on the level of feeling. As that is my personal persona I suspect he evoked strong countertransference as the holder of the feelings. During one of the last sessions when I was trying to explain to Kevin why I could no longer be visiting on a regular basis, he countered by saying I came to visit Joe. "But I also have got to know you during all this time", I said. "Yes I know" he replied, "and you know me better".

Following my final visit we arranged a get together for about a month's time, resisting Olga's offers for me to visit or drop in on weekends. Kevin phoned me one Saturday morning to tell me that Joe had started to walk. Olga had forgotten that it would be a month before we met again and phoned to see if I would like to drop in one Saturday.

All this leads me back to my final task, which was to connect this experience to the consideration of the place of young child observations on a DipSW course.

In many ways the effect of the course was to reaffirm what I knew already: the validity, and crucial role of observation in social work. Unlike psychoanalysis, where the observation vantage point I suspect can remain relatively intact, in social work, prescriptions are essential elements of the role. But performance-prescribed tasks without observation are skewed at best, and damaging at worst. Especially if sufficient attention is not paid to countertransference.

25

Thus definitions of social work could perhaps include being an observer of self as a participant, and the dynamic of the interaction between clients and workers in the wider context.

More broadly, it helps students become aware of process thinking and how much more goes on in every interaction than meets the eye.

Part II
The Context of Observation

3 Paul: At a university nursery   29

4 Jenny: Blaming the victim: A two-year-old's experience   38
   of an institution's defences against anxiety

5 Sophie: Managing an adult agenda in a middle   45
   class family

Introduction

The three essays in this part take the reader into the worlds of Paul, Jenny and Sophie, magnifying the joys and pains of childhood. They draw attention to the dilemmas in modern life explored more fully in Part IV and the emotional demands of observational studies on those providing day care. The focus is the impact of where children were observed.

The experiences of Paul and Jenny in day care, surrounded by many other children and looked after by many carers, contrast sharply with Sophie's life at home with her parents. By contrast, although Sophie spent most of her day-time in a nursery, she was observed at home. The presence of other children and adults during the observations influences perceptions and the childrens' behaviour.

The authors cannot ignore other issues in the observational environment, an example being the total quality of care provided for all children. Paul's and Jenny's lives in day care are presented as different in quality, although the distortions inevitable in the observation process need to be kept in mind. Jenny's observer became her ally, sharing her agonized feelings associated with the process of change.

Sophie's world, too, has unanticipated pains, reminding the reader of how parents develop styles of parenting reflecting their own needs and experiences. What may initially seem a critical picture of Sophie's life is, from the observer's perspective, both revealing and thought-provoking.

For readers struggling with the question: What is good enough parenting with all its personal issues? these essays make an unusual contribution to the debate.

3 Paul: At a university nursery

There have been two moments of particular significance in my observation of Paul and the group of young children who attend the university nursery alongside him. First, towards the end of the observation period I arrived in the nursery to find Paul sitting astride a long, sausage-shaped cushion. He was addressing an explanation, as ever, to both himself and to anyone who might be engaged by it:

Paul: This one's number eight

After the routine reminder by Daniel (one of the nursery children) of my place:

Daniel: "Did you see my daddy?"
Me: "No"
Daniel: "How long have you been here?"
Me: "Two minutes"
Daniel: "No you haven't"
Me: "I have. How long have you been here?"
Daniel: "Three minutes!"

I am drawn back to Paul who has travelled across the room astride the cushion:

Paul: "I want to tell you something in a minute"

This was addressed to those assembled in general, and then repeated specifically, and with increasing insistence, first to Charlie and then to John and Walter.

He continues:

"One day I'm going on an electric train first, then an underground train, then an Intercity with my dad!"

Then following a pause:

"Here come the underground trains!"

The other boys proceed to the firehouse in the corner of the nursery unmoved by Paul's announcements.

Paul presses on to the story corner noisily and with energy:

Paul: "I'm going to Birmingham Station. Number eight Birmingham train!

Here comes the underground train – watch out for the train!

It's coming! You're on the railway and here comes the train!"

There is no observable response:

"My train's on fire, call the fire brigade."

The fire brigade, in the form of Walter, John and Charlie, immediately arrives and the fire is extinguished following a sequence of drama and incident.

The boys disperse and Paul continues, with reflection, to shuffle around on his train.

Here, it seems to me, we have a young boy, rising four years in age and in his final pre-school year, negotiating for himself and with his peers a new and exciting social identity in the real world of rail travel through the familiar procedures of fantasy play. The fire brigade and their hoses remain the make-believe they have been all year, representations through which exciting yet safe social roles and identities can be inhabited by the children as they create and recreate social relationships and culture. Paul, however, while using the cultural norms of his peers to gain their involvement, is preparing for a different level of participation in the social world beyond the nursery and the firehouse.

Secondly, several weeks before this episode, while reflecting on the social competence of Paul and his peers in the nursery and on the rich culture they created for themselves through their play, I came suddenly upon Walter with his mother and her friends crossing the campus lawns. I found myself instantly shocked at his small size and the impression of vulnerability which it provoked in this 'adult' context. I became troubled about the possibility that I was investing in Paul and his peers capacities and competence beyond their developmental potential when I observed them together in the nursery. Placed in the wider social world, Walter had his childishness dramatically restored and his dependence on his mother and other adults was apparent. I was reminded how reliant on them he was; how ephemeral the cultural process the children created in the nursery.

These moments have been important in helping me to make better sense of what I have learnt about both the emotional and social development of small children and the experience of observing that process. They prompt divergent thoughts and emotions which are taken up and rehearsed in the written notes and the observation seminar. For example, because the observer is influenced by postwar discourses on child development they can find themselves witness to the processes of damaged development in emotionally deficient environments. Drawn, in the observation, to the rescue of vulnerable children, but properly careful in containing both role and emotion, the observer uses the seminar to work through the impact of having privileged access and exposure to the child's experience while being prohibited from intervention that might alter or ameliorate it. Much of this process of exploration comes to focus upon the centrality of the dependence of the observed child on caretakers and on the extent and nature of their responsibility for a child's emotional health and social well being.

When I first planned to observe Paul in his day care setting, I chose the first hour of the nursery day on Monday, partly because, in this frame of reference, I imagined my thoughts and feelings would be taken up by the issues of separation as primary parental carers handed children on to substitute day carers. The assumption here was that the behaviour and emotions of the child might be attributable directly to the quality of the parental or substitute care and of the transition between the two. The social relations and emotional content of the nursery could helpfully be seen in the image of a spoked wheel. The attachment of each child to the 'parental carer' (family or day substitute) at the hub would determine the quality of the child's experience. The main point of interest would concern the age and developmental stage at which a young child could best manage the transition between family-based and substitute attachments. The relationships between the children themselves would wholly derive from the individual adult/child attachments. The observer would be seeing these attachments and their impact as played out in the child's social relationships. Where the child was left emotionally unsafe by poor family or day care attachments the observer might be expected to associate with the child's distress. Being unable to act upon this association, the observer would carry it for examination into the seminar. The examination would, at least in part, implicate three different categories of caretaker: (1) caretakers of the child (2) caretakers the observer had had to rely on in the past and (3) the observer as the caretaker he or she had been or still was.

Seeing Walter so small and dependent outside the nursery made me realize the extent to which I had ceased to make sense of my own observation of Paul, Walter and the others in this way. Rather than being drawn into thinking about separation and substitute day carers, I had come, by that stage, to adopt and present a highly appreciative and celebratory stance in respect of the social world produced in the nursery by Paul and his peers. As I experienced, recorded and discussed the resourcefulness of the children and how fertile and exuberant their efforts were to produce their own culture, I had come to see them as bigger than they were. The integrity of the social world they actively constructed each Monday morning through play, language and the use of educational and other props and the identities and social selves they developed served to emphasize competence and self-determination. Rather than feel a need to intervene and protect or rescue, I occasionally wanted to join in and play with this humorous, expressive and adventurous group of children.

On this account, Paul and his peers are engaged, through codes of language and/or play, in making active use of a variety of resources available to them in order to establish a social self and social identity or identities. Resources include social representations of the roles and identities open for adoption whether in fantasy (say Batman) or reality (a fireman, a rail traveller); social space as is afforded by a nursery and its facilities, and facilitative caretaking relationships which provide emotional and social security. Cultural creativity rather than developmental vulnerability becomes the focus of observation.

In what follows I try to organize my understanding of what I observed in the nursery by holding social, cultural and developmental considerations in mind. I hope to show that it is possible to celebrate the efforts and achievements of Paul and his young friends in producing their own growth and development while not forgetting how small they still are, how they construct their identities through a constant interrogation of social and emotional objects and what responsibilities this confers on the adults who care for them either at home or in the nursery.

"Paul is quite an independent lad"

It is a hot and sunny June day and the children are outside. Paul is considering what to do next. Hands in pockets, he hoists up his trousers and surveys the scene. He has tried out both the red tractor and the rocking boat, but he has not felt able to settle to either. As he stands in contemplation of his next move, Steve (a nursery worker) discusses his perception of Paul with Rose. It is an impression I have developed myself from the start of my visits to the nursery.

We agree that Paul does indeed make an observer feel at ease – he does not present many loose ends that need tying. He seems to have this effect on his peers too and they are often drawn to him – Angela and Emma at the beginning of the year, John, Stephen and Walter later on. And while Adam's long periods of isolated concentration trouble me from time to time, Paul's pensive absorption in solitary activity convey what I describe at one point as "a powerful stillness and gentleness". In the sandpit he digs his hole with care, precision and persistence; with the water pump his face is marvellously expressive, tongue pressed on lip, head tilted as, patiently and with enormous interest, he finally works out how the device works – *"They pump water don't they – when you push that down."*

This facility to attend, and achieve satisfaction through it, is also occasionally extended, on occasion, to social interactions. Early in the observation period the children are crowded round the 'playdoh' table and are engaged in feeding the stuff to a collection of plastic dinosaurs. I note, with reassurance, the happy combination of crowded yet collaborative play.

As if on cue, Daniel takes Paul's dinosaur, a large one, and on being asked by Nita, he throws his small one to (almost at) her. Paul contemplates this process and after several seconds says to Nita, "Are you small?". Here, like me, Paul seems to have sensed the potential threat to the co-operative accommodation reached by the children which is posed by Daniel's directness. He is able to register yet contain the impact this has on him and, in some way, attend to Nita's experience as well.

Later in the year Paul is renewing acquaintance with Walter after a long summer break. Within seconds of arriving he is engaged in an excited, giggly discussion with Walter over a Captain Pugwash book. As ever, the legitimacy of their experience needs verbal confirmation:

"These are very funny stories!"

They discuss which character to be in the book:

Paul: "Well I'm a soldier. I've got a sword as well."

Walter: "He's helping that man."
  Paul: "He's a kind boy, isn't he?"
  Walter: "Shall we look at another one?"
  Paul: "No"
  Walter: "Yes"
  Paul: "Yes"

Here we find Paul alongside Walter in both a physical and emotional sense. It is important to Walter that Paul is with him and one senses that Paul, not Walter, will decide when it's time to move on. Yet Paul takes notice of his friend, confirming Walter's experience.

Paul, then, brings to the nursery and conveys, by his behaviour and presence in it, an emotional centredness and personal integrity.

Paul: "Jo, can I please have the steering wheel?"
Jo (worker): "Share it with the boys"

The nursery, or at least the hour a week when I see him there, provides a set of contexts through which he actively develops this emergent sense of self. Throughout the year I watch as Paul and the others explore and consolidate personal and social identities through play, in dialogue with self and others, by the manipulation and exploitation of games, toys and social props and all this in ways patterned by both available space and time.

Much of this is rich and creative, compelling to this observer in whose eyes these small children grew surprisingly large and who often wanted to join in (rather than organize or rescue). A pageant of cultural production unfolded in recurring patterns of play as the children inhabited and interrogated roles made available to them in the social representations of the wider world.

In observing Paul and his peers, I realize I find myself watching an active process of cultural production and identity formation and yet one in which the children are always checking out the real boundaries of the world they create and recreate and which provides their real contribution to their own development. The children constantly remind themselves (and others) where these boundaries lie, what the 'rules of the game' are. In this way, they seek to confirm that the adults are, after all, still properly in charge, able to contain that all too familiar sense of vulnerability.

Paul: "I'm going to tell Steve!" (worker)

Occasionally adult boundaries need to be readily invoked, but this is rare. In many ways Andrew's dismissal of his father early in the year is illustrative.

Andrew's father is concerned not to rush away without settling his son who seems to want him to stay:

Father: "I'll play for a minute."
Andrew: "Five minutes." Father: "OK" (stoops down)
Andrew: (immediately) "You can go now"

Reassured by his father's attention, Andrew instantly feels safe enough to let him go.

In general, the children in the nursery make use of the nursery workers in this way. Occasionally I feel a little irritated on behalf of a child whose need for a more active or sensitive response from a worker seems to me to be unmet, but it is usually the children themselves who elicit sufficient adult support.

Laura arrives at the 'playdoh' table, apparently bent on disruption. She seizes Paul's 'playdoh':

Paul: "Not all of it, not all of it!"

In irritation and distress, Paul firmly places his hand on the remaining lump in front of him and looks up and over to Rosie (nursery leader) for support. Rosie has understood the situation, walks across and suggests that Laura takes a smaller amount. She does. Play is instantly restored.

New boy: "Kill, kill, kill!"
Michael: (who had been at the nursery for a term) (quietly in passing) "We don't have any guns here."

A great deal of the children's play is rulebound. This is a further way in which the children make safe the experience of imaginary play through which they make for themselves social identities. Rules are invoked by the children more often than by the workers. In the incident here Julia, the worker, overhears the exchange and comes over to reinforce the message with the new boy in a way that leads to a discussion about pretend and real killing. Even then, it is Luke himself who explains to Julia that he was only pretending to kill the monster.

It seems important to Paul and the others that play is made both legitimate and safe. They constantly negotiate these dimensions in various ways as they try out social identities and roles represented in the adult world while hanging on to the comforts of make believe.

Paul: "Fergus! I was playing with that thank you very much".

It was always important to Paul that he had access to significant social props which he used to facilitate individual and joint play. Paul seemed especially centred, firmly located in his projects, when he had a possession to hand. He was quite vulnerable on occasions when he foresaw or experienced the loss of this object, as if his identity was at risk without it. This applied both where these social props enabled him to enter a microworld, e.g. a crane, play people, and where they enhanced an adopted role, a police hat. In the course of the year, Paul hung onto a shop till, a chair, a crane, a helicopter, play people, a spade, a calculator, a bow and arrow, a tractor and a police hat.

When props were secure, identity could be explored as this note records:

I watch Paul, who is in reflective mood, choose something to carry in the trailer of his tractor. As he drives past his thoughts escape in a little whisper to himself, "I've got a police hat ...". He instinctively touches the hat – just to make sure.

Paul: "I'm getting this right now, right now, right now ... I'm getting this right now. There we are!"

Paul is talking to/with himself, confirming the authenticity of his organization of the railway track and engines. This authenticity seems to relate to both the achievement of a valued social role or mastery of a game and to a state of emotional security. Paul and the others "thought out loud" a good deal in singleton play or where it was necessary to give voice to an explanation which perhaps validated and made bearable an uncomfortable experience.

So when Paul slides down the pole in the firehouse and falls a little heavily he says *"That was quick, that was quick!"*. Likewise on falling from the swing Marian seems to contain the mild surprise of her jolt with the reassuring explanation *"There we are, we've come down bump"*.

In my notes I referred to these and many other episodes, as self dialogue – a talking to oneself employed by these children who, being alone, needed to account verbally for their experiences and thereby authenticate them. However, the existence of the "we" in many of the incidents makes the notion that children play in the presence of a parent quite compelling. "We've come down bump" is so unmistakably parental.

Angela: (quizzically) "Would you like to marry me?"
Andrew: "Not today thank you, because we're playing firemen."

This brief encounter encapsulates the central elements of the children's social role play. Roles and relationships are negotiated through conversations and explanations. They are also quite distinctly gendered with the boys routinely, but not exclusively, adopting and developing active public roles based in the real (fireman) or fantasy (Superman) worlds available to them, while the girls usually (but not always) explored domestic identities. The latter could include mothering – often the dolls but sometimes the boys themselves.

Angela, in particular, is keen to offer emotional succour whether feeding Peter as a baby, partnering Hugh ["I'm your new boyfriend, I've got braces"], or welcoming Walter back from a (very) long period of being "dead". ["Darling, you're better at last!"].

On two occasions gendered and care giving play became consolidated in rather less whimsical enactments. The first, on a wet and blustery day in July, concerned family violence as my contemporary notes record.

Paul, Stephen and Fergus are developing their game in the upper floor of the firehouse which is reached by a staircase and can be descended from on a pole running through the floor. This floor provides the ceiling for the lower part of the house in which Angela, Daniel and Adam become engaged in more domestic pursuits.

I hear talk of marriage from the playhouse. Angela soon emerges dressed in lace and sequins and heads for the firehouse where Paul is already playing:

Paul: "And when the bells go we have to slide down the pole."
Angela: (In the lower part of the firehouse) "But don't land on my baby will you, else I'll be cross ..."

Stephen arrives.

"Don't Stephen"
"Stephen!"

Adam and Daniel join Angela and play 'babies' in the lower part of the firehouse. Paul, Stephen and Fergus play fireman above.

"Don't Stephen!"

Adam curls up in a ball on a cushion. Angela is saying something to him which I can't hear.

Paul slides down the pole.

Angela: "You're not fighting in our house!"
Paul: "No, we're firefighters but we don't fight. We're coming to the rescue."

Paul and Fergus continue to play noisily up and down the firehouse and pole while Angela, Daniel and Adam curl up on the cushions and converse. I move nearer but can't hear them for the noise of the boys. I wish Paul and Fergus would shut up!

Fergus: "Good evening!"
Paul: "Bad eve ... it's a bad evening rescue!"
Angela: "The baby!"

She moves across to the black doll lying near her.

    Daniel: "I'm the baby!"
    Angela: "No"
    Daniel: "Hit it."

He bashes the baby hard on its head with his clenched fist. He then sets about wrestling with Adam who is the dog.

As the violence escalates in this family, Rosie (nursery leader) comes across to check things out.

However, mediation is not enough...

Daniel is in discussion with Angela:

    Angela: "Only if you don't smack my baby ..."

Daniel strokes the dog's head before moving across once again to threaten the baby. This seems the final straw for Angela. She throws herself dramatically across the baby in a gesture of desperate protection.

    Angela: "I'm going away, I'm going away - with my rucksack!"

She gathers up her bag, the cushions and the baby and sets out to leave the house just as the firefighters appear to the rescue

For this observer the unheard accommodations and negotiations of the private domestic sphere which fail to prevent the vicious outbreak of violence while all around is clamour and diverting activity is utterly riveting, yet quite awfully disturbing in its familiarity.

The fights by the boys for control which seem to be at the heart of this episode are repeated a few weeks later when gender identities again get apparently threatened.

Daniel has been playing a game involving the pushing of babies in buggies with Nita and Angela. I realise this is beginning to trouble Paul, Walter, Stephen and Andrew in the firehouse.

They first ask Daniel if he is a fireman. He says he isn't. He can't play then ... But of course he doesn't want to play and that is the problem.

So next the boys get mischievous and decide to capture the buggies. This plan is implemented rather reticently and ineptly and soon dissolves in failure.

The boys draw Daniel into a "silly talk" game but he remains imperious and proceeds in his play with the buggies and dolls.

The boys seem unsettled.

Stephen and Dominic follow Daniel to the playhouse but soon return to the firehouse.

Andrew invites Paul to join him in play "We're fireman monsters, let's go and scare people".

Stephen and Walter play together.

Stephen to Andrew, "We're going to spoil your game".

Later Daniel arrives at the firehouse without buggy or doll. He is promptly expelled by all four boys.

As the year proceeds and I get to know Paul and the others much better, my awareness of both gendered patterns of play and of individual differences in the personal and social identities of the children develops. In some of these episodes the incipient tyrannies of the school playground and beyond are, perhaps, momentarily glimpsed – patterns of aggression and victimization given, fleetingly, social form. But this is exceptional and although Daniel is a black African boy, I don't experience my reactions to the observations through the discourse of 'race' and 'racism' in this multi-ethnic setting. Instead the "monstrous" behaviour generally appears to belong elsewhere, in that childish need to test the boundaries of risk and safety and build a sense of personal security through recognition of the distinction between imaginary horrors and the real world. Paul and Angela demonstrate the art:

Paul emerges from the playhouse running, excited, clasping and swinging his arms, grinning, "We play Little Red Riding Hood!

They play out an elaborate game. Paul is especially animated:

"I ate little pigs!"

He looks at me and our eyes meet. He jumps up, addresses me with some insistence:

"I'm a friendly wolf!"

Like him, I'm reassured.

Christine:(nursery worker) "And how are you this morning?"
Daniel: "I don't know!"

The process of observation asks the observer to attend to the child's experience and operates through both emotional response and intellectual reflection. The consolidation and transfer of learning from the experience of attending observantly requires, above all, time and good questions. The seminar groups and the period of writing this paper generally provided for both in the same way. The nursery seemed to deliver safe time and space for Paul in which he and his friends could ask themselves those questions which consolidated and transferred their learning and helped them to make sense of themselves and their own experience at a transitional stage in their lives.

4 Jenny: Blaming the victim:
A two-year-old's experience of an institution's defence against anxiety

This paper attempts to bring together the dual experiences of a two-year-old girl and the staff of a day nursery when faced with the trauma of separation from a known caring figure. The choice of a day nursery for the observation stems from a professional interest in group care. The child selected was not previously involved with any social work agency, other than medical or health services.

I first met Jenny when she was 18 months old, the only child of a single parent. She attends a social services day nursery on Monday and Tuesday of each week, having been referred by a health visitor who thought that Shelley, Jenny's young mother, needed a regular, short break from the full-time care of a toddler. Shelley gave her permission for me to observe her daughter.

The observation began after Jenny had been attending the nursery for four months. In my first observation, when I arrived early enough to see Jenny and her mother enter the nursery I noted:

A young woman in her late teens or early twenties came in with a fair round little girl. She is plumpish, fair haired with large brown eyes which are always watchful of whatever is happening around her. Jenny is standing in front of her mother, reaching up to her. Shelley is holding one hand, while talking to the nursery nurses about their weekend. Jenny constantly reaches up to her mother, who continues to talk to the staff. She turns to me and says, "she's alright when I've gone".

Shelley and Jenny are brought to the nursery by taxi from their home about six miles away. The nursery serves a large geographical area which consists of a string of small industrial villages. A high proportion of children travel to the nursery by taxi; frequently two or three mothers and their children travelling together. This is an important feature of Jenny's day at the nursery as she may experience a considerable physical as well as emotional distance between herself and her mother, knowing mother will be whisked away in the taxi after making their goodbyes.

Most of the observations were made on Monday morning between 10 and 11 Sometimes they were later, over lunch or early afternoon, just occasionally I observed Jenny at the end of her day when she was collected by her mother. This pattern has meant that I have been privileged to observe and reflect upon the meaning of transfer from one environment to another, in the first instance from home to the nursery and in the last three months the additional factor of settling into a new nursery group with a new keyworker. This latter stage is the focus of the paper.

Jenny had been attending the nursery for just under 12 months when her transfer to another group room was planned. The nursery is organized around three groupings of children and a small group of babies and their parents. There is one group for under twos and two large groups (about 20 children in each) of two to four-year-olds. All children are allocated a keyworker who has her own 'family' of children. From my observations the children spent very little time if any within the 'family' although the keyworker is responsible for recording her key child's daily progress and maintaining links with the parents or other caretaker. Jenny's first year in the nursery was spent within a setting of no more than eight children at any one time, with two nursery nurses, frequently supported by students. Jenny's transfer from this small group was to be part of a general system of planned care for all children.

Before describing the transfer it feels necessary to give a picture of my experience of Jenny as a little girl suffering some anxiety about being away from her mother and needing to communicate what this separation means to her. From my first day she developed several games and interactions involving objects disappearing and reappearing. I was an easy target, being more or less static, the only adult not involved in other children (or not initiating involvement), clearing up, or setting out games and toys. On my first observation I noted:

... Jenny walked away from the table, looked at Shelley's toys, came back, pushes a chair underneath the table, looks at me directly, and clearly says "gone". I respond by joining in with "gone", and "there it is". This game is repeated several times.

The following week similar interactions take place:

Jenny comes over to the table, another child is nearby holding a book for me to look at with her. Jenny joins us, puts her hand over another book and says "gone" - she then picks up a further book, holds it under the table and says "gone", picks up a third book in her other hand, drops it and says "gone".

These games of objects disappearing and reappearing are played quite regularly, sometimes the objects are placed inside a box or other container. In later observations Jenny hides herself in corners behind cupboards or curtains. She also initiated a regular interaction in relation to her clothes and "mummy", indicating Mummy had dressed her or bought them for her. An example of this during the nineteenth observation when the children are eating breakfast progressed as follows:

Andrew, a two-year-old, is looking at me in an enquiring way then returns to eating his apple. Jenny turns towards me, her eyes wide open, touches the sleeve of my sweater, pulls the cuff of her own (just like two weeks ago) and says "Mummy". She also tugs at the body of her jumper – I say "did mummy put your jumper on?" Jenny says "yes", – then says "mummy gone", my response is "mummy has gone home?", "mummy brings Jenny to the nursery?" Jenny nods her head, says "yes". She then gets out of her chair, walks a few feet away, turns, looks at me, and again tugs at her jumper, lifts it a little, says "mummy". She is looking at me seriously, it is as though we are having a real grown-up conversation ...

I am surprised time and time again by the repetitiveness of these 'games' and communication between Jenny and myself, and frequently experienced a tug-of-war between my role as observer and wanting to assist Jenny to fill that empty space she would seem to carry during these first hours in the nursery. These episodes indicate a deep need within Jenny to express externally the internal process of preparing to come to the nursery, of her arrival, mother's departure and a wish for reassurance that her mother will return. A further feature of Jenny's behaviour in the small group room is her watchfulness of all activities, especially when someone enters the room, and a tendency to play at the edges of the room, usually by herself with dolls and a cot. Her favourite place is inside the doll's cot. Jenny has a good relationship with the nursery nurses who are genuinely fond of her, but the routines and emphasis on providing stimulating activities does not allow for much individual attention, and even less opportunity to observe any child's daily experiences.

Within this context a firm decision was made that Jenny was old enough to transfer to the buttercup room; that she was ready for 'older' and more educational activities. The usual method is for children to make a series of 'visits' to their new group over about two weeks. I am told they usually move smoothly from one stage to the next. Three other children had already moved on within the space of a couple of weeks.

Jenny's first visit to the buttercup room was just before Christmas when she was taken by her keyworker, Angela, for a short session. Angela stayed with her and brought her back to the daisy room. In the New Year other 'visits' were arranged on each of the two days Jenny was in the nursery. The initial visit accompanied by Angela progressed according to the norms of the nursery, until the day Jenny was just delivered and left to play without the familiar presence of her keyworker. I am told she became distressed and returned to the daisy room. An observation during this period illustrates Jenny's willingness to be the compliant child, to do what is expected of her, but the 'good child' is then overwhelmed by an awareness or sense of abandonment; fear and anxiety:

When I arrived Angela tells me Jenny is in the larger nursery room. "I've just left her, she's not crying." Angela seems flustered and anxious. (We have a lengthy discussion about whether I should observe her or not and decide with the senior nursery nurse that it should go ahead as usual.) Anne (senior nursery nurse) takes me to the buttercup room. Anne and I enter the room together, Jenny is directly opposite in the home corner organizing a small rug. She shakes it out with a corner in each hand, just as she shakes the sheets of the doll's cot, then carefully lays it on the floor, smoothing it out with both hands. As she stands up she sees Anne and me, rushes forward past Anne, myself and two other nursery nurses, towards the door, calling out "Angela" in a tearful, anxious voice.

Two weeks later Jenny is still in the daisy room and the following observation takes place at the end of lunch when Jenny is eating her pudding.

Angela asks Jenny if she is going to sleep in the buttercup room, Jenny says "no" in a clear loud voice, and then what sounds like "go in Angela's bed". Angela gives a grumbly grunt and speaks to me above Jenny, "she wants to go in Angela's bed!" Angela turns to Jenny and says she could sleep with Sally and Andrew (the two children who moved earlier) in the buttercup room, but again Jenny says "no" in a firm voice, and continues to eat her pudding.

Later during this observation hour Jenny asks to go to the buttercup room and runs off happily followed by Angela and myself. As we enter, a nursery nurse is about to read a story to a group of children: other staff are clearing up after lunch, there is an air of being very busy:

The story nursery nurse half-turns and with a big surging movement reaches out towards Jenny who has run over to her, but then Jenny swiftly turns around, calling out "Angela, Angela" several times, in a panicky fearful voice, her face full of distress, puckered up, tears falling. (My perception was that Jenny panicked on a realization that she was about to be 'swept up' by the very cheerful, bouncy nursery nurse.) Angela lifts her up, turns to me and says impatiently, "I can't leave her now; it's not the right time, but if it were less busy I'd leave her here".

During these weeks staff were anxious to keep me informed of Jenny's behaviour in relation to their attempts to settle her into the new group. She was described as wilful, difficult, strong willed, manipulative. Staff expressed amazement at this block to an expected smooth transfer of a child. It interested me and often saddened me that no one queried these 'smooth transitions'.

On what became Jenny's last day in her familiar base, the observation indicates the way anxious threat was used. I was already aware of a gathering sense of frustration and even doom around the issues of this transfer:

During the parting session, Silvia a nursery nurse from the buttercup room comes in with a little girl. She stands at the door, calls out to Jenny asking if she's coming to play with Kirsty? Jenny turns and says "yes, play in room", in a friendly voice. "Come on then", says Silvia. It is then Jenny realizes what it is all about and vehemently says "no", looking down at her picture. Silvia persists, calling out (she's still standing near the door, a good distance from Jenny) "come and play with Kirsty", Jenny says "no", and then in a very distressed voice, calls out "go away" her face flushed with an upset expression. She shouts loudly "go away", several times only looking towards Silvia with the first "go away". After that she shouts it out, while looking down at her picture the whole time. Silvia calls out "well you're coming tomorrow". Jenny then looks at her again, quickly, her face still anxious frowning, her lips moving but no sound. Silvia leaves with another cheerful "see you tomorrow". Jenny returns to her picture, putting her finger in the glue, testing it very carefully - she's serious ...

This episode is followed by another only a few minutes later, where Jenny spontaneously undresses herself to be weighed, after watching another child have his nappy changed. She has not been undressed and weighed for several weeks as she is now too heavy for the 'baby' scales.

Jenny steps up on to the mat, sits down, glances at me, looks towards Angela very smiley – I can almost feel Jenny about to lie herself down, poised ready to be 'babied'. Angela now looks at her, surprise in her voice, "what are you doing sitting on the mat? you haven't got a nappy to be changed?" ... Angela lifts her into the tray of the scales. Jenny sits there looking around her, very pleased with herself. Angela laughs at her, exclaiming that she looks as if she intends to sit there all day. Jenny certainly looks pleased with herself – the most contented while I have been observing her that morning.

41

The final separation of Jenny from her base in the daisy room and from Angela her key worker was made in (I believe) a draconian fashion. When Jenny's mother Shelley collected her daughter on Monday afternoon, she was told that the next morning she was to take Jenny directly to the buttercup room, and not to stay! Shelley was most obedient – she left Jenny quickly, whereupon I am told Jenny screamed and cried for two hours. The following week she protested again but for a shorter time. When I saw her in the following two weeks she was quiet and serious.

My first impression is that she looks tired, and even that she has just woken up - her hair looks uncombed and sticking close to her head, her face pale and puffy ... She looks across at me with a serious face, makes no signs of recognition, other than her long slow glance, eyes meeting. She has a cold and a runny nose. She sits eating her pear slowly, not interacting with anyone ...

Later in the morning I observe she walks to the bathroom in a 'flat feeling' way. It was a long time on that morning before I saw the smallest smile on her face.

I believe the nursery nurses want truly to care for the children in a loving way and that they have strong affectionate feelings for them. When reflecting on Angela and Jenny, I see a strong bond and realize that Angela as substitute carer also experienced feelings of sadness and loss, which were unexpressed, even denied. Nevertheless, there appeared to be little understanding of the seriousness of the transfer or the significance of relationships to a small child.

In an attempt to make sense of my observations and the comments made directly to me by staff, I turned to the work of Isabel Menzies Lyth (1988) and some action research in a nursery by Andrew Bain and Lyn Barnett (1986).

Menzies Lyth's research and consultancies have centred around hospitals, therapeutic communities and other health services, including a day nursery. One area of interest to her is the way institutions defend themselves against anxiety and the inevitable denial of feelings within both the patient-client and the nurse-worker. She writes of defensive techniques in the nursing service which enable a nurse to protect herself from anxiety by splitting up her contacts with patients, by never nursing the 'whole' person and by her time being filled with mundane tasks. Menzies Lyth (1988) shows how the anxiety stems from the nature of nursing very ill, injured or dying people which can arouse primitive, infantile needs to be cared for oneself. This anxiety is further compounded by the nurse introjecting the patient's feelings of distress, sorrow, anger, depression and anxiety. If the nurse has actual early experiences of separation or neglect her work with 'needy' people may also reawaken long ago feelings of pain and hurt. This is supported by Bain and Barnett who found that many nursery staff in their project had as children 'experienced abnormal experiences themselves', which they associated with the nature of the relationship of the staff with the children (and with high staff turnover).

These explanations or findings, provide a context into which the nursery staff's behaviour towards Jenny makes a remarkably neat fit. It provides an explanation for what I sometimes sensed was a loss of ability to deal with a situation which has advanced beyond the nurse's control. If Jenny's distress and fears of abandonment aroused earlier unresolved primitive fears of rejection and of infantile experiences of hate and anger within the nursery nurses, Jenny must have taken on the stature of a monster: hence the labels of wilful, self-willed, manipulative. Perhaps they are in fact mild descriptions compared to the felt experience. Is this why Silvia, her new key-worker, could not move closer to Jenny when she brought Kirsty to invite her to play, remaining safely beside the door? Menzies Lyth (1988) clarifies such projection by workers in helping professions by explaining how infantile phantasy* situations are projected into current work situations and experiences.

"She then re-experiences painfully and vividly, in relation to current objective reality, many of the feelings appropriate to the phantasies. In thus projecting her phantasy situations into objective reality, the nurse is using an important and universal technique for mastering anxiety and modifying the phantasy situations." (page 49)

I find it necessary to remind myself that not only would the nursery nurses introject Jenny's anxiety, but in projection of their phantasies, she in turn would introject the nursery nurses' strong feelings of anxiety and distress. She must have lost any sense of being contained and held, her world of the nursery deprived of safe boundaries and bereft of an adult to interpret her feelings and experiences for her. (In the third week following her permanent move, I observed Jenny stuffing tissues into a cup, putting lots of concentration into her attempt to fill it as firmly as possible.) In trying to grasp the totality (or as much as possible) of Jenny's experience it was very supportive to find Bion's concept of the "capacity for reverie", (in Menzies Lyth 1988) linked into my understanding of Menzies Lyth, Bain and Barnett (1986). No one among the staff of the nursery would seem to have grasped this concept or made time for reverie, so Jenny did not experience it.

"a mother who would accept and introject the projective identifications ... and through her loving relationship with him, return them freed of their terrifying dread and anxiety."

During a recent observation I was impressed by the contrasting responses of Jenny's new keyworker to a sick child whom she was tending in a very gentle way, to her more curt, controlling and dismissive responses to Jenny's distress: "she's just having a paddy". The sick child was passive and accepting, confirming the nursery nurse's desire to love and care, whereas Jenny's anger and fear would seem to stimulate hostility and projection of the dangerousness of relationships?

Bain and Barnett (1986) observed that the system of care in a day nursery was:

"organised partly as a defence against the experience of the nurse of intimacy with the children, and in particular as a defence against experiencing the child's psychological needs, pain and disturbance."

They identified the psychological pain for under-threes as consisting of intense distress caused by long and repeated periods of separation from their mother or other main attachment figures, together with the impossibility for the under-

---

* The term phantasy is a psycho-dynamic technical term for unconscious phantasies to distinguish them from the conscious fantasies of imagination.(See also page 52.)

threes of forming an adequate relationship with a substitute attachment figure in the nursery because of absences and high staff turnover, and where relations with adults are marked by intense competition and rivalry with other children.

In the case of Jenny's nursery there was not a high staff turnover, although there were frequent and different additional helpers, and Jenny did make a close relationship in the daisy room where she competed with only six or seven other children for the attention of two adults. However, it would seem that neither Angela nor Jenny's attachment to each other was recognized, or at least, it was accepted as easily transferable. Bain and Barnett noted the denial by their nursery of the uniqueness of individual nurses and that it did not recognize that children and nurses may be significant to each other. In the buttercup room where 17 to 20 children share the attentions of four permanent nurses and an occasional peripatetic helper the opportunity for Jenny to make a similar attachment was severely diminished. The keyworker system as presently operated did not appear to lead to a significant adult being available to each child.

At this stage, almost the end of my observations, I was aware that Jenny was caught in a double dilemma within the institution's defence system. At the point of transfer she had still required help in unpacking her feelings linked to the departure of her mother, and separation from familiar surroundings and people of the previous five days.

She was spending her days at the nursery in a watchful mode rather than engaged with the other children and activities. Her attachment to Angela was the one positive element in her long 'wait' to be collected by her mother at the end of the day.

Jenny's transfer from one base to another cannot be seen as successfully completed until she forms a secure and significant relationship with a nursery nurse in the buttercup room. Unfortunately because she is part of a system which does not recognize attachment and intimacy as important features of day-to-day interaction between children and adults, it will be left to Jenny to find a replacement for Angela. In recent weeks I have observed her attempts to form new bonds between herself and individual members of staff: once with a young student when they played feeding a doll, and more recently reaching up to be lifted by a nurse. The following extract from a recent observation indicates the size of the task facing the two-year-old as she begins to adapt to the expectations of her new caretakers.

Jenny wanders away from the climbing frame and goes over to the nursery nurse who had previously lifted her up, raising her arms to be lifted: the nursery nurse does so, but then puts her down again without seeming to say or 'do' anything. I find Silvia (present keyworker) is near me – Jenny wanders over, taking off her coat which she hands to me. Silvia says to Jenny "you're very quiet this morning: perhaps that's because I haven't spoken to you yet!" (Jenny has been in the nursery over an hour).

5 Sophie: Managing an adult agenda in a middle class family

During my time practising and teaching in child protection, mistreatment of children has been seen as arising from extreme emotional, physical and environmental circumstances. Because of these pressures, adults' agendas may so totally eclipse the needs of children that a child comes to be viewed and treated as an object.

In making a number of observations of a nine-month-old girl in a 'normal' middle class family I expected to observe a child's emotional development in the context of 'good enough' parenting. And so I did. There was no sense that the care of this child came anywhere near the threshold criteria laid down by statutory agencies as to what constitutes abuse. Quite the contrary, this child was well looked after and had devoted parents. However, the sequence of observations showed that the child-adult relationship, while not actually abusive, showed in much less extreme form some of the same dynamics. In particular, the caring adults had a persistent tendency to impose their agenda upon the child without being aware of the child's need and right to do things their own way.

I want to explore how this emerging pattern revealed itself; reflect on my reluctance to acknowledge what was happening, and consider how the child responded and developed ways of coping emotionally with the situation in which she found herself.

My understanding of what was emerging from my observations was given some structure by the concept of "container/contained" originating from Bion. While I do not want to embark on a full discussion of Bion's thinking in relation to this concept, I will indicate briefly the aspect of his thinking which I see as relevant to this paper.

In order to develop an internalized ability (mental apparatus) to deal with emotional and mental pain, a child needs her carer to be able to 'contain' the good and bad feelings she expresses. Containing means a carer having the capacity to receive the emotion the child expresses, hold onto and think about it, and then respond to the need in a way that the child can manage. Over time, with a mother who responds in a 'good enough' way, the child internalizes the relationship with the mother as the capacity to manage discomfort within herself without needing the external mother to relieve her all the time. If a child regularly experiences a denial and distraction of her feelings by her carer, then she does not internalize a good experience of a holding mother and needs to resort to other strategies to manage her powerful feelings.

I shall refer to some of this thinking as I explore a number of themes arising from the observation material. These include: first, a consideration of the style of parenting and the parents' expectations, including the need for their child to be constantly active; secondly, thinking how a child learns to wait; thirdly, how a child learns to cope with separation and a lack of emotional containment;

fourthly, how a child learns to control her situation; and fifthly, a consideration of the nature of her relationship with the observer.

To outline the context of the observation setting, the observations began when Sophie was nine months old. She is her parents' first child. Her mother is white English and her father is of Far East Asian origin. Both parents have professional jobs and are in their early thirties. Sophie's birth was not difficult. At the age of six weeks she was placed in a nursery since mother was returning to work. The home is comfortable with a garden.

The adult agenda

I want to consider the practical and psychological context created by the parents for Sophie's upbringing. My understanding of this context has been primarily shaped by observing Sophie's interactions and behaviour during 25 observations over a period of eight months. During this time I was also given information by the parents which added to the picture.

By examining what I have termed the adults' 'agenda', I do not intend morally to criticize her parents for adopting their particular style of parenting. Rather, I want to reflect on the setting which will enable me to understand how the child made sense of her situation.

Due to the varying demands of his work, father occasionally saw his daughter consistently for days at a time and sometimes not at all for a period of days.

Culturally he seemed content for Sophie to be brought up mainly in an English milieu. However, he was also keen that she should gain some familiarity with his language and so frequently used it when speaking to her. Mother supported this approach.

Both father and mother acknowledged that father had a relatively strict upbringing and that he tended to encourage stricter limits and requirements of behaviour of his daughter. While mother laid less rigid boundaries, there appeared to be no schism between her parents regarding attitudes to child rearing.

At the time the observations began mother was starting a full-time course of study. This required Sophie to be in a nursery five days a week for most of the day.

It seemed to me early on in the observations that mother felt pressurized both in terms of the demands on her time, and the mental demands of the college work. The juggling of timetables and arrangements for Sophie's care were a feature in the background of many sessions.

Adult-initiated activity

But if mother was not always available emotionally to her child (Bion's container) it was not necessarily and only due to her mind being full up with these external demands on her. After a few observations it seemed to the seminar group that there was another dimension to the adult carer-child interaction, and that both parents were working to the same agenda. Observation sessions were characterized by constant activity of the adults' making, not initiated by the child.

For instance, during the fifth observation:

While Sophie was sitting down and still turning her teddy over and over, mum moved some of the furniture and lined up the brick buggy. She then lifted up Sophie and took her over to the buggy, placing her upright with her hands on the handle. Sophie then took steps forward pushing the buggy in front of her. Mum said she had started doing this on Sunday. Sophie was smiling broadly while concentrating intently. Mum turned her round and Sophie walked back to the other side of the room. Mum set her up again and Sophie did it again, stumbling a little with mother catching her.

On the face of it this seems an unremarkable episode of a parent encouraging and stimulating their child to begin walking. However, it is also illustrative of a constant tendency to require the child to do something; to be involved in some activity. There were few occasions during the observation period when Sophie was permitted to just be and follow her own rhythm.

This is illustrated again, more starkly, in the third observation, when dad was caring for Sophie, who was tired, constipated and unwell:

Dad sat Sophie up against the activity centre. Sophie was still crying, rubbing her eyes. Dad went through each activity encouraging Sophie in a lightly joking way: 'Here comes the little person's eyes' or 'Press the nose and up pops the head'. Sophie stopped crying and watched intently. Dad went through the actions two or three times. Then he got up and went to the other side of the kitchen to put on the kettle. Sophie continued to look at the activity centre, reached out and turned one of the dials. After a few seconds she turned and attempted to crawl towards me ... The effort seemed too much for her in her present state but she still tried. She carried on crying. Dad came over and sat her upright and brought out the plastic bear and turned his dial. Sophie went quiet while she watched.

This extract shows a child whose feelings of exhaustion and unhappiness are handled through distractive techniques; the child's discomfort is not absorbed, contained and reflected back in a more manageable form for her.

Child as a 'project'

It seemed to me that the fact that Sophie sometimes seemed not to be offered an emotionally containing experience, particularly when distressed, was in part related to a parental view of the child as a 'project'. The adults have expectations that the child will achieve certain developmental milestones according to a certain schedule. This in turn gives rise to an anxious frame of mind in monitoring the child's progress. So there develops a tendency for the parents to relate to the child in terms of her 'performance' and achievements. The fact that their child was their first born may also have increased parental anxiety that 'everything should be all right'.

Again, Bion's thinking (1984) is relevant here in that a child will not experience her carers as containing if they are parenting an 'ideal' child in their heads. They are doing their best to parent a child, but not the one in front of them. They may have an image of how a girl should develop and behave; they may carry a lot of cultural baggage from their own experiences and backgrounds. The upshot is that because you are full of your ideas of how the child should be, you are not attending or listening to the actual child in the family.

An extreme example of the need to ensure that Sophie (aged 13 months) developed at the 'right' pace in the right way was the occasion when I arrived for an observation to find dad holding her firmly on the potty in the living room while she cried and struggled to get off it. This went on for about two minutes, then dad released his grip and Sophie crawled away from him.

By the sixth and seventh observations the pattern had been well established that the observer had come to watch Sophie performing and being engaged in activities set by the parents which showed how she was developing. The performance on the brick buggy was a regular feature for about five consecutive observations. And there were other achievements to be shown:

Mum said she wanted to show me how Sophie manages to get off when placed on the sofa. She placed Sophie flat on the sofa. Sophie manoeuvred herself round so that she was going head first over the sofa edge. Mum guided her round so that her legs went over the sofa first. Mum repeated this exercise. Mum took Sophie over to the green glass bottle with plants in it. She said "Sophie likes to stand by it looking in".

The fact that there is constant activity while the parents are with their child can mean that a style of parenting develops which does not emphasize physical and emotional closeness and reflectiveness. Even at times when there is close physical contact these can be dominated by singing and bouncing games. The significant issue is, how does Sophie manage and come to terms with a reality which she appears to have little capacity to influence or control?

Saying 'No'

Another important factor in defining the climate in which Sophie is growing up is the parents' attitudes and actions to saying 'No'.

During one observation (at 13 months) I watched Sophie take an interest in some pot plants by the french windows.

She went up to them and touched the leaves. Dad said 'no' sternly and moved her hands. Sophie touched the leaves. Dad repeated word and action. Sophie touched the leaves. Dad smacked her hand and said 'no', more loudly. She also looked in my direction. Dad smacked her hand again. By this time Sophie was very distressed. Dad picked her up and put her in a pedal car. Dad said on another occasion Sophie needs to learn 'no' as well as 'yes'.

While mum's handling of boundaries may not appear so openly disciplinarian, her actions are likely to leave the same confusion in the child's mind when 'no' is given as a response without explanation. For example, in a later observation when Sophie (16 months) can walk:

Sophie followed mum into the garage. Mum manoeuvres Sophie away from the garage door and says "You can't come in here, it's Daddy's garage". Mum then brings out some tea and ice cream onto the patio. Sophie follows her and indicates with her eyes and hands that she wants some. Mum gives her a taste but it is too cold and Sophie refuses. She then looks in my direction and comes over to my table. Mum emphatically says "no". Sophie goes back to mother and has a bit of ice cream and this time eats it ... Sophie looks in my direction and makes towards my ice cream with mum saying "no" sharply. Sophie stands looking at me and pulling at her straps.

Mum's sharp negatives are in contrast to her soft communication just prior to her injunction. This seems to accentuate the 'no negotiation, no explanation' manner of establishing limits. In Bion's terms, an opportunity is being lost here of helping the process of thinking for Sophie. She has no means of learning why a boundary is being set at this point. She is left with an understanding that adults have power and the magic to decide when she can do something and when she cannot. So the problem posed for her is how to gain some measure of control and not be left completely helpless in the face of this magical, arbitrary power.

A child's way of managing emotionally

By discussing what I observed to be some of the important themes in the parents' approach to their relationship with their child, I do not intend to give the impression of the child as a passive recipient of adult impositions. On the contrary, in exploring how Sophie manages her reality, we can see how she is able sometimes to negotiate changes in that reality. Certainly, she develops ways of making it bearable for her emotional self. However, it is important not to lose sight of the child's position in relation to the power of the adults and her more limited number of choices in coping with her situation.

A major issue for Sophie has been: how does she cope with separations and the non-availability of her primary caretaker?

From an early age Sophie had experienced long periods of time separate from her mother. From the start of the observations it was evident that Sophie would take full advantage of mother's availability whenever it was offered. In the first three or four observations I observed her hang onto her mother very intensely, trying to bury herself in her mother (10 months). While there was a sensuous element to her actions, there appeared also to be a desire to control and hang onto mother:

Mum knelt down beside Sophie and picked her up on her right side. Sophie climbed up mum putting her face into her mum's neck, then moving up and putting her face in her hair and pulling it very hard. She was making excited panting noises. She then moved round and touched her mum's face, moving her fingers across her nose. Mum said that Sophie had been at nursery each day that week and seemed to be content there.

Yet, she also seemed to be a child who had learned how to wait and deal with her feelings without disintegrating when the person she wants is not available. She had learned to hold onto what she had got in a controlled and concentrating way. In this sense she used her curiosity to interest and hold herself, blinkering out the fact that her mother is coming and going. For instance, later in the same observation:

Mum then put Sophie down in front of the sofa, putting the activity board facing her, with the shaker bottle and a plastic book. Sophie looked at each toy as it was put in her range. Mum then left the room to make tea. Sophie did not look up after mother. She took

49

the crinkly carton and pressed it in her hand making a sound. She then reached for the shaker bottle which was out of her reach. She leaned forward and with assured balance moved back to a sitting position. She held the bottle by its end and shook it and let it fall between her legs. She then picked it up again to shake it. She didn't look in my direction. She picked up the end of the plastic book and turned it about, occasionally putting it into her mouth ...

She is learning very fast how to manage her feelings of being in the room with a stranger and wait for her mother to return by concentrating intensely on an activity. This was a feature of the first three months of observations, before Sophie could walk and be mobile.

Establishing some way of controlling her environment in order to cope with her feelings seemed to be a constant theme during the period of observation. This pattern was observed in a later session when Sophie showed again that she could manipulate and concentrate on objects as a way of dealing with her feelings of loss and control.

At this point Sophie (10 months) is very tired and is "holding out".

Mum took Sophie over to the toy area and placed her with her back to a large mirror on the floor. Sophie was grizzling desultorily during this. But when her mum pulled out the activity set and started showing her some activity objects she looked carefully at what her mum was doing. Mum then left the room. Sophie did not look after her, nor did she look in my direction. She leaned forward and began manipulating the different objects, particularly a plastic roller which she moved deliberately with her separate fingers. At one point she made a small cry but generally she concentrated silently.

One way of coping with one's feelings of loss of control can be expressed by the idea of constructing an alternative structure within which one feels safe. This becomes necessary if mum is not experienced in a containing, holding way. One session illustrated this vividly:

Mum said to me disappointedly, "She's not doing her cupboard routine today". Sophie turned and started crawling fast and confidently in my direction. She didn't get up to me but started to go under the bar of the buggy, trying to get up and inside. She cried out when she found herself unable to do this. She pulled back and tried again to crawl underneath. Then she pulled herself up to the tray of the buggy and balancing herself used both hands to pick up the yellow duck and put it in her mouth.

It is possible to perceive Sophie trying to get inside something structural (in this instance, mechanical and inanimate) when she feels mum is not available in an attuned way. When that attempt fails, Sophie puts an object in her mouth to contain her feelings. I return to the implications of this process in a moment.

At the same time, this was also a period when Sophie regularly experienced colds, coughs and small physical ailments. For the first four weeks of observation Sophie experienced constipation, which may have been her way of coping with external changes. Examples of these are mum less available since the summer; the regular visiting of a stranger; occasionally being looked after by dad rather than mum. The tense retention of faeces may have been her way of holding her feelings in check, expressing them bodily.

In the early period of the observation she seemed to accept the boundaries set by her carers and pursued her activities within the limits set. However, once she had a taste of being with her mum for a prolonged period when she was ill at Easter, she was no longer prepared to accept without protest her ration of mother's availability. She was by this time able to walk with full agility (14 months).

The contrast for me as observer when I saw Sophie after a break of a few weeks was striking. I encountered a child (14 months) who clung onto mother with great determination and would not let her out of her sight. Mother said this had been the longest time she had been with Sophie since she was six weeks old. She was experiencing Sophie's 'clinginess' as pressurizing and was hoping that this phase would not last too long.

Sophie demonstrated how determined she was to hold onto and control her mother:

In the kitchen Sophie is holding onto mum. Mum picks her up and tries to put her in the highchair. Sophie resists and kicks her feet. She holds onto mum's neck. Mother puts her down and Sophie holds onto her legs as mother goes to the other end of the kitchen. All the while she is whining and clearly unhappy ... Mum picks up Sophie and tries to put her in the high chair again – Sophie kicks and protests ...

It is possible that during her ill period she experienced mum in a containing way and now she is fighting to retain that. But if mum is not there to hold her then she needs to find an alternative structure to hold herself. If she does not, then she can be left with feelings of being overwhelmed, out of control and uncontained. This seems to be an issue that Sophie is struggling with in different degrees of intensity during the observation period.

Sophie sits on mum's lap. She sits up and leans forward and picks up a crumb off the floor and puts it in her mouth. She does this again and mum notices and encourages her to pick it up and eat it. Sophie gets off mum's lap and stands by the high chair and starts indicating she wants to get into the chair. Mum says "Good girl" and lifts her up – Sophie slips her feet in.

A possible interpretation here is that Sophie no longer feels contained by a mother who lets her scavenge, she is feeling out of control and she wants to be somewhere safe like the structure of the high chair.

The proposition can be expressed: being helpless is emotionally awful, so pretend you have control over inanimate things which will not let you down. If the worst possible thing is to feel lost and alone, then the task is to create a coping structure which is strong enough to ward off those feelings.

The problem arises when the containing structure regularly becomes an inanimate structure and not a person. In an earlier observation we saw Sophie resorting to putting a duck in her mouth to contain her feelings. Both situations show up the potential danger of using an inanimate object permanently to deal with feelings. Instead of being person-connected you switch off from being person-related to being thing-related.

Another dimension to Sophie's struggle to deal with a lack of emotional containment by parents and their demand for constant performance-related

51

activity was her relationship with the observer. In the early observations she had to make sense of this strange person who did not respond to her in the way that other people generally did. This was a source of emotional confusion and seemed to be dealt with by her great capacity to concentrate and use her curiosity in her play things which we observed earlier.

However, by the second month of observation it seemed to me that Sophie realized that the observer had a space in his head for her. This was a person who regularly once a week attended to her. He was not someone wanting to do things for her or to her or put things in her mouth.

For instance, there was an occasion when early on in an observation session mother explained to me that Sophie (10 months) had a cold and had not slept very well the night before. As mum talked, Sophie:

... looked at me directly and kept her eyes on mine. She seemed flushed, her eyes watery and her nose a little runny ... As mum talked, Sophie continued to look at me and did not move in her mobile. Mum said she was going to the kitchen and Sophie would follow. I waited for a few moments. Sophie did not make a move and kept watching me. I then started moving out of the room and Sophie made short whining sounds.

At the beginning, it seemed to me that Sophie was 'fixing' me in a way that enabled this strange but attentive person to stay the same between the last session and this one. In this way a person can be 'controlled'. One does not have to deal with the complicated business of where they have been in between then and now; and, if one wasn't getting their attention, then who was?

Further into the interaction it seemed to me that at one level Sophie was focusing on the observer in such a way that she was hoping for her discomfort to be relieved by this person who was focusing on her intently.

At another level, Sophie's relationship with the observer became the ground over which she struggled to work through the tension between externally imposed limits and internalized boundaries. The question posed in one seminar session was: will she explore the curiousness of the observer or will she have internalized that here is a boundary she should not cross? In other words, can you explore your fantasies* and ideas, or is this not permissible? Do you make do with what is given and laid down by adults?

Mum gave Sophie a wooden spoon which she turned round and round, end on end for some minutes, sometimes looking in my direction and sometimes making whiny sounds but remaining in one place. She then moved the buggy towards me but made no attempt to go up to me and touch me. She carried on manipulating the spoon, this time putting the stirring end in and out of her mouth and sometimes turning it around. She turned her back on me and continued to do this. I got up and moved around her so that I could get a better view of her face. I stood in the doorway. Sophie looked at me and continued to stare at me, as if waiting for me to do something.

It seemed to me that the issue for Sophie here is: does she explore the boundaries of the situation set down for her or does she try to explore beyond them? The presence of the observer seems to be a containing boundary for her but it is

---

* See footnote on page 43.

not clear in this instance whether this is a result of her self-imposed limits or externally imposed boundaries.

To conclude, in this paper I have discussed some aspects of the climate and boundaries established by the parents in their relationship with their daughter. I have gone on to consider some of the issues and ways in which the child responded in an active, not passive, way to the situation she found herself in.

Sophie was an intelligent girl who found herself in a situation where she not only had less of her mother's time than she appeared to want, but also had to deal with day-to-day boundaries imposed on her as a result of the parents' image of the child they wanted her to be. I have looked at two aspects of the way in which this girl set about coping with her reality. I have not looked at a number of other ways in which she dealt with her feelings of being contained or uncontained, such as her reactions to food and eating. However, it seems to me that the material shows the size and complexity of the task a child has in making sense of and 'surviving' the hopes and expectations of her parents when they are imposed in a 'non-negotiable' way.

The generally subtle and 'culturally normal' way in which this adult agenda was imposed meant that I as observer took a long time to begin to recognize what was going on. As the observations and seminars developed the process highlighted issues around the tension between the imposed adult agenda and the strategies the child developed in managing this agenda. This experience has made me reflect on my own parenting of my three-year-old boy, and the way he resists and accommodates the agenda I impose on him. It has also helped me reflect on the way in which I was parented in the early fifties.

Part III
The Cultural Context: observing difference

6 Thomas: a journey into a different territory   57

7 Bina: Observing cultural difference   66

Introduction

Social workers attempt to acquire skills in culturally sensitive practice in accordance with the requirements in the Children Act 1989 to take into account children's 'race, language, religion and culture'. Child observation presents a unique means of developing knowledge and skills in this area. The following two essays demonstrate the complexities of the dilemmas presented.

They portray vivid accounts of how cultures become altered and blurred in the process of time and by the movement of people round the world. Thomas and Bina's lives are shaped by the cultural contexts in which they live. The extensive kinship systems which nurture them during their early years provide the observers with rich learning opportunities. Thus, the observer has the opportunity to learn about specific cultures; their influence on childrens' development; and the relevance of this experience to other practice situations. Above all, the writers scrutinize their subjective reactions to their observations and, through discussions in the seminar groups, present a useful account of their own process of learning.

In the words of Bina's observer "learning from weekly observations is so vast it leaves you gasping".

6 Thomas: a journey into a different territory

The family whose child I chose to observe and who agreed that I could come into their home over a period of almost a year to observe him and them, came originally from Southern India. Although they had lived in the UK for a considerable time, they had only recently moved into the district where other members of their extended family lived. They all formed part of a small and fairly tightly knit group of Christian Tamil families. The doctor who put me in touch with this family described the community as self-contained and family-oriented.

I knew little about Southern India, most of the families I had encountered had come from further north or were refugees from the war in Ceylon. I was informed by a close friend who came from the area that traditions were strongly observed and that the transition to a twentieth century mode of life for a middle class family could be traumatic, as it had been for her. I had been immensely touched by an Indian film which portrayed beautifully not only the strength of family ties but also the powerlessness of a once influential Brahmin class who, in the course of tremendous social upheavals and reforms, had remained rigid and become helpless. The film captured the dignity and sorrow of one family in the face of loss and was set in a landscape which seemed timeless, very green and intensively cultivated, so that the permanence of seasonal changes introduced a note of movement and hopefulness.

I felt a sense of excitement, like on a journey into a new territory.

After I had introduced myself to the family they checked out my credentials and reassured themselves that I was undertaking this observation with the purpose of adding to my knowledge and understanding of children. Their high regard for education assured for me their total co-operation. I felt always very privileged and while initially like a square peg in a round hole when I entered their home, their welcome and light-hearted acceptance of me as an observer helped me to develop the appropriate stance and to remain 'actively passive', that is to retain a physical distance, while allowing myself to become deeply involved (Trowell 1991).

Entering their home was like entering a different world which was both physically and emotionally contained and containing, separate from the outside, rarely intruded into by phone calls or visitors; a world which was so much closer to what I imagined it to be like in India than to the home I came from. And yet there were also all the similarities: the modern kitchen, furniture, appliances, open doors and carpeted floors throughout, books, pictures, plants, toys, television; daily routines like children going to school, parents going out to work and grandparents who stayed home to look after the baby during the day and the older brother and his cousins after school and during the holidays.

The parents were in their thirties, had been educated in England and spoke English when alone with their children. But Mary, the mother, who had been born and raised in India, and her parents-in-law, spoke her native language and taught it to the children so that there was a constant mix of languages, the native language being more frequently used for commands and instructions or emphasis, particularly by the grandmother.

They had two boys, Jason then aged five, who attended the local primary school, and Thomas, just 14 months, who had literally 'found his feet' and was enjoying this new and exciting state of freedom through mobility. He was a sturdy little chap with an impish smile and the curiosity and urge for exploration and testing out which was eagerly observed not only by me but also by his grandparents and every other adult who happened to be around. The older brother and two cousins, Matthew and John, were often told to humour him or give way, which appeared to raise few protests.

The grandparents lived with the family during the week only and returned to their flat in another part of the town at weekends, "though the children always want to phone them", said Mary, and grandmother added with a broad smile, "there is never any peace from them". She seemed older than I later learned she was, but still agile and swift in her movements, always watchful and quick to intervene in order to avert or prevent any danger, mishap or potential conflict. When Thomas uttered one of his piercing screams because he could not get what he wanted, others were told to give it to him or he was distracted. Grandfather seemed more peripheral to the child care task, but could be used as ultimate sanction, just like father, either in person or as a threat; he was observed to be good as mediator and comforter. On the whole, however, there appeared to be very little cause for sanctions, and major conflicts did not seem to arise, not in my presence at any rate, and not as an undercurrent which was in any way perceptible to me.

From the outset I was impressed by the grandmother's centrality and her total dedication to the child I observed. As the observer of an infant who seemed so central, and became, perhaps, even more central through my presence, I felt increasingly drawn into this comforting and cossetting environment and happy in a world that seemed so secure and protected. It was an opportunity to get back in touch with unconditional love and acceptance, to suspend judgement and hand over responsibility with a sense of relief; particularly after a harsh day back at work. I had no difficulty in letting go of the professional adult at all.

There were times when Thomas wanted to open the front door and go out into the world as would be normal and consistent with his development. Each time he was brought back I felt a mixture of sadness for him and gladness for me, who identified with him, as I knew what it was like out there.

The seminar group, who listened to my descriptions, were less enchanted by the pictures I drew and critically examined my sketches. While I was still at the stage of allowing the environment to act on me, and reporting faithfully, my colleagues increasingly saw things differently. Questions were being asked about the emotional development of the child, his opportunity to gain greater separation and individuation; the grandmother's role in the family generally was questioned. Who was his primary attachment figure? How would he achieve self-confidence and autonomy in the outside world when he was so shielded and protected? Was this a culturally determined socialization process or a specific trait of this family?

I became increasingly perturbed and exasperated with not being able to paint an accurate enough picture of the environment in which this child grew up and which to me seemed very good on all counts. What was happening in this group? Were they envious? Was I blind? Insensitive? We did not seem able to resolve this at the time.

I was more preoccupied at that stage with the impact of me, a white person, on Thomas who at times gingerly touched my legs but on the whole kept his distance as I kept mine. His mother and grandmother always walked barefoot in the house, though only his grandmother wore traditional saris. My skin is much whiter and I wore shoes which he had also recently begun to wear. What was he thinking? What was his perception of colour difference and, more importantly, its meaning? Not only was my colour different but also my language and my unspoken communication to him through looks and movement.

My presence had an impact, but how could it be assessed in the context of the observation? He seemed a securely-based child, but where did he pick up the cue to be so careful about not involving me for longer than other children I had known? Was this because of my colour, my observer stance or some communication he had picked up from his mother and grandmother?

The seminar group had correctly noticed that I was enjoying the observation and its atmosphere; but I wondered whether their apparent difficulty in accepting what seemed to me to be a culturally different but functional style of child rearing was due to envy, or perhaps prejudice.

From time to time I felt a little like a stranger in the group, and slightly persecuted about presenting as I was not sure how my family would be perceived. It made me think about otherness and being a foreigner, not only because I had come from a different country myself, but also, because I felt protective of this cultural difference which was not like my own but one with which I had become closely identified through the observation. This relatively confusing and mirror-like situation continued until well into the second term.

I will now try to describe the process through which I, and the seminar group, eventually reached a better understanding of what may have been happening in the course of the observation during what I perceived to be three different phases.

There was the initial phase, during which I tried to find myself in the observer role and establish a comfortable distance. Then the middle phase, which lasted roughly until after the Easter break, during which I tested out various hypotheses, looked at attachment issues, emotional factors and normal events in the context of this particular family. In the final phase, the questions arose again relating to the social and cultural characteristics in the environment. They are briefly discussed in the light of what has been observed and in comparison with some research findings from India.

Initial Phase: finding myself as observer

My decision to undertake the observation seminar was partially the result of having some available time but mainly the fulfilment of a cherished wish to be able to observe without having to pass judgement, to be able to record and log patterns like an artist for drawing or painting, and to allow shapes to emerge by themselves, gradually. Several accounts of previous observers, and things I had read, re-enforced this wish, and raised a slight anxiety that it would be difficult for me to remain passive in a family setting where people, and particularly small children, normally reach out and request interaction and social activity.

The family I observed was very helpful in keeping the boundaries we had agreed initially. At times it seemed that there might be too much control on the older boys, who were discouraged from interfering when the toddler attempted to join their play and upset or damaged something. It was usually grandmother who sorted it out. I gained the impression that noise was discouraged and that conflicts, so essential for the experience of a resolution, were avoided or bypassed.

An example follows:

Thomas, who at 15 months was interested in hard objects, keys, knobs, beakers had been given a bunch of keys by his grandfather when he asked for them. He put them in his mouth which was noticed by his grandmother. "Dirty", she said, "give them to me, don't put them in your mouth". The commands were repeated several times without result. Thomas looked at her and at his grandfather and continued to bite on the keys. Both patiently tried to cajole him, laughing initially (thereby giving mixed messages to him), then more seriously to persuade him to give up the keys. It might have developed into a game but remained a serious contest, or so it looked from Thomas's point of view. Eventually grandfather found a music box and wound it up to divert his attention. He invited Thomas to dance with him, grandmother joined in and the keys were dropped as all three danced in the hall."

As an observer, who felt closely identified with the infant in this intense drama, I rejoiced that he had been given an opportunity to be taken seriously; that he did not have to become angry but could give up the keys as irrelevant when something more interesting was suggested. I had also been interested in the verbal and non-verbal cues given by both adults and the kind of detailed reciprocal interactions, particularly those between grandmother and child, which were similar to those described by Daniel Stern (1985) as "attunement", and which were an integral part of a larger action, as here.

The child looked at his grandmother holding tightly onto the keys; she looked back at him as intensely, raising her eyebrows and pursing her lips; he put the keys to his mouth; she lifted her finger to the height of his or higher without taking the keys saying "no"; he shook his head; so did she, saying "no, no", always looking at him, almost encouraging him to resist by staying with him, lending him support almost.

Yet another part of this interaction, I observed, was the grandmother's intention to stop Thomas from screaming. I had seen her give in, bribe, cajole, threaten mildly, tell fibs, anything in fact, to get Thomas to give in or give up, rather than actually confront the conflict, by being firm. She must have been uncertain how Thomas would react here, yet certain that she would not let him scream, which may have transmitted itself as message, through her body language and the tone in her voice and may have been the stronger message, as conflict was indeed avoided.

Conflict avoidance became the subject of the seminar discussion as did concern for the apparent lack of opportunities to learn about confrontation and hard objects. What stopped me from being able to state that there need be no concerns?

Looking back I do not think there was total absence of conflict or lack of opportunity to make a mess, but there certainly was less than there would have been in a comparable western household. As there were always at least two adults on call, the children had learned to play independently, but usually with a minimum of noise or fuss. There was a strong trend towards conformity but within the context of much patience and constantly available adult attention.

From the toddler's viewpoint life had few frustrations as almost all his needs were met. My total enjoyment of this different world and the whole experience of being a privileged observer rather than a professional assessor stopped me from wanting to judge or infer meaning from an adult's perspective. Yet the identification with the child was strong and felt good because, alongside the pacification and control, there was also a lot of instruction to participate in whatever was going on, to play, observe, name and identify things, to be useful and to join in some of the games of the older brother and cousin.

Because it seemed 'good enough' in Winnicott's sense, my own very basic needs were allowed to be attended to in a way which put me quite powerfully in touch with early experiences, good and not so good, particularly with my losses and everything that contributed to the loss of what had seemed a similarly protected and secure early childhood.

These were some of the reasons why I was not concerned. The other reason, I think, was my failure to give a sufficiently fine grained picture of my observation. Having now read some of the accounts of other observers and commentators (Miller, Rustin *et al.* 1989; Stern 1985; Brazelton and Cramer 1991) I realize that my informal assessment and judgement of what was 'good enough' was, in fact, less informed by the kind of interactions described above than by the pattern of communication between the child and various family members. This communication, particularly between grandmother, mother and child was coherent and consistent, and conveyed unspoken messages about approval, rejection, modifications, affirmation. I had also failed to give detailed descriptions of the level of autonomy and flexibility this child had achieved (Brazelton and Cramer, Chapter 14) and the signs of his secure attachment which at the time the observation began was probably mostly to his grandmother, but must have been to his mother earlier as she was very important, though in a different way. He seemed to go to his mother at times of fear, upset or need for comfort. He would seek out his mother when bored or in need of reassurance, although this pattern did not become really apparent until much later.

Middle Phase: testing hypotheses

The family went to India in January for a visit to their relatives on both sides and in both generations. The excitement just before the departure practically eclipsed Christmas which, apparently, is not as important or commercial a festival for them. Nevertheless, there was a Christmas tree and presents, 'so that they don't feel left out', explained Mary.

On returning Thomas's brother, Jason, who before going away had spoken a very clear, slightly stilted Queen's English, now spoke with a strong 'Indian' intonation. Thomas sounded to me as if he was imitating the intonation of a language but without actual words, although I was told there were some clearly recognizable words. He clung to his mother and would not leave her out of his sight. When I arrived they were both upstairs 'hoovering' (huhu, he called it). Thomas, unbalanced I think by my sudden appearance, hid behind his mother's skirt and peeped out from behind her legs. Only gradually, through a lot of eye contact and checking and watching while I talked with his mother, did he re-establish contact with me, and then wanted to demonstrate how he could help her carry bits of the vacuum cleaner downstairs.

Grandmother appeared to have moved to the background as far as Thomas was concerned. He wanted to be with his mother. There was a scene, when Thomas and his mother, almost like a pair of lovers, sat on the floor and seemed involved in some game which brought them very closely together, with Mary matching him in his activities; singing, talking, pointing. The closeness between them was new to me but seemed so naturally grown that it must have had its roots in the beginning of their relationship.

Mary told me that Thomas had been with her constantly during the six weeks in India, that he now hardly left her side and that he demanded to be carried all the time. 'There are so many people in India, children get lost if you do not carry them all the time', she said. He had been poorly and had lost weight as a result of stomach upsets.

I was interested in what seemed a new phase, a regression in some ways, as Thomas was more clingy, yet would have to endure a separation from his mother as soon as she returned to work. Would the old pattern re-establish itself? He was 18 months old now, seemed younger because he was small, but was developmentally in advance of the average in language and skills. During the following weeks I particularly looked at the mother-son relationship and, as part of that, his emerging sense of self, which seemed to be present in that first encounter after their return. The observed social interaction and Thomas's understanding of his mother's teasing seemed to have reached a new level of self-awareness in terms of reciprocal play, understanding and a sense of wanting to be more consciously, teasingly, assertive and wanting to experiment (Kagan 1981).

Another observation comes to mind, when Thomas, angry about a prohibition his mother had imposed, flung himself into her, pounded her face with his fists and screamed with a degree of anger that I had not observed before. His mother calmly held his hands to protect herself and him and persisted in her course, holding him and his rage until he was exhausted. There were many other instances when it became clear that the quality of relationship between Thomas and mother had reached a new stage and that this appeared to have been happening at his instigation and her response, rather than on her initiative. His grandmother told me that he now 'demanded' her presence; presumably his worry about being left or stranded had intensified following his first big journey.

My responses during the observations after their return were also somewhat different. I began to see the child and his family from a more detached position and found myself thinking much more analytically about the meaning of behaviour, allowing myself perhaps to be less impressionable, less 'lost in reverie'.

Thomas continued to have illnesses during this period, measles, colds and more colds. He took refuge in his daybed, a plastic boat-like structure with a softy rounded rim over which he flopped to get to his blankets and cushions. He was often asleep when I came. His grandmother also began to look very tired and there were times when I felt a sense of loss and sadness during the observations, which remained vague but noticeable in a lot of little transactions, tone of speech, moods. Grandmother told me on one occasion how she missed India, particularly in the winter, but little more was said on the subject. Mary once commented that she thought Thomas went to sleep so much because he was bored as there was little for him to do during the day. Soon after that grandmother and Thomas started to attend a play group in the morning.

Final Phase: social and cultural questions re-appear

Mary started Thomas's toilet training shortly after Easter, and accomplished this within a relatively short time and without apparent fuss or difficulty. He was 19 months, which is late by Indian standards (Bassa 1978). Thomas was proud to let me know that he now knew how to be in charge of his bowels and staged a number of false alarms. The only area where Thomas still appeared to be lagging behind was in his eating habits; he apparently refused proper solid food, despite having healthy teeth, still used his bottle and needed to be goaded and coaxed into eating. His grandmother and mother commented on this, smilingly, and wondered why, as the older boy had eaten solids much earlier. Someone in the seminar group hypothesized about food being the last bastion for making a stand, now that toilet training had been accomplished. I was not sure, but wondered whether, from a systemic point of view, there was a family dynamic at work which delayed Thomas's progress towards solid food. I had observed that none of the caretaking adults in the family ever persisted with conviction in getting Thomas to eat regularly, or to eat what everyone else ate. Unlike with toilet training and cleanliness, he got his way with eating chocolates, and having milky drinks and snacks almost on demand. On one occasion I saw grandmother hand feed the four year old cousin, Matthew, out of a bowl of rice while he was watching television. Was this a family or a cultural pattern? Grandmother's role in the family seemed to be largely defined by her child-minding activity. Presumably she carried this out in the way she had been raised and to the best of her ability. So why the discrepancy between what was being said and what I observed?

I found an interesting paper by Bassa (1978), who worked in a community mental health centre in Bombay for 20 years and systematically followed over a 100 infants over a period of 15 years. He comments on common threads in both middle class and working class families. There is, he states, a cultural tendency in India for adult carers, mothers, aunts, grandmothers, to adulate and overprotect their infants and to prolong infancy "through on-demand feeding and delayed introduction of solids, excessive body contact and carrying, sleeping with the mother or other caretakers", so that "the end result is a curious admixture of unbound trustfulness, to the point of gullibility, mingled with sudden and unexpected reactions of mistrust". He makes the point that there is a lower rate of child abuse probably because "mother and child are shielded from each other's aggression and provocativeness by others who intervene, divert, bribe or comfort as the situation demands". He claims that the transitional stages, in psychoanalytic terms, are denied to Indian children because there is little opportunity for physical, bodily separateness and the sublimation of powerful impulses, like aggression, into play, resulting in "unintegrated impulses and unresolved problems relating to dependency, sense of achievement, self-esteem, self-assertiveness, individuation, control and sublimation of aggression". I cannot help but think that this is a list of all the attributes highly valued by Western civilizations. I also wondered about the function of a 'prolonged childhood dependency' in a country where food is scarce, spaces to live even scarcer and where there are so many people that, as Mary said, children get lost, unless carried.

It was interesting however to find so many similarities in Bassa's description and to hear almost all the sentiments, which the seminar group had expressed, confirmed. He concludes his article wistfully by stating "Mother India does not easily let go of her children. She safeguards her youth against violent change by keeping them dependent and conforming".

The following extract from one of the last observations illustrates the shifts that had occurred in Thomas's life and the things which remained the same:

He and his cousins Matthew and John were huddled together on a couch while the grandparents were watching television. Mary was in the kitchen with Jason who needed to do his homework. John was looking at a book. Thomas tried to wrestle with Matthew, who wanted to watch the film. He gripped him around the head almost strangling him. The grandparents were aware and said things like, "careful Matthew, leave him, don't ..." until both boys rolled off the couch and onto the floor where Matthew allowed Thomas to pound him, barely protecting himself. The grandmother was still asking Matthew to stop but did not put the kind of firm emphasis into her voice which would convey a message of intent. Although I felt a sense of protest on behalf of both boys and wondered how Thomas would process information that so blatantly ignored his display of prowess, I also realized that neither of the boys actually took much notice of what their grandmother had said.

Thomas gradually lost interest, got up and ran to his mother in the kitchen where he began to interrupt a close encounter between her and his older brother. In this little episode Thomas succeeded in getting his brother away from his mother, which suited both of them. He was tired of homework anyway and quickly joined the others in front of the television. Thomas was left with his mother who now showed him a book of pictures and, at his insistence, had to read or explain every page, without skipping.

In the seminar group where I had long stopped feeling the outsider, everyone expressed relief that this little chap was showing all the usual signs of a healthy, well-balanced toddler, attached to his mother and very fond of everyone else. His socialization was preparing him for the outside world, nursery and school in a way that no longer raised concerns about his ability to cope.

Implications for social work training?

Families dependent on the support of large extended families can become extremely vulnerable and stranded if this support is not available and not recognized by the host culture (Ahmed, Cheetham and Small 1986). Here, however, the support system was intact and maintained through the close-knit community. There were signs that the toddler was over-protected by western standards, but there was also sufficient elasticity in the system to provide future opportunities for a gradual transition to the outside world. The danger of isolation and defensive rigidity was thus avoided. Any assessment, just like the observation, needs therefore to be placed in its wider social context.

I am still puzzled by the guarded watchfulness that Thomas observed towards me until well into the second term, which may or may not have been related to my colour. It was only through the establishment of trust between his adult care-takers and myself that he eventually allowed himself to come closer. It might have been interpreted as 'clingy' or as insecure attachment, though this would stretch the imagination. The important point is one made repeatedly in the literature on child observation: it is the ability to suspend judgement and to allow oneself to become responsive at every level, which is so useful. But it needs a seminar group or good supervision to provide the necessary detached and, hopefully, balanced view.

It is important to establish through observation what constitutes a good enough fit between a child and its carers and whether differences are working for or against the child's healthy development. In this case, the balance very likely swings in favour of this little Indian prince. There are other young people, whom I encountered at later stages in their lives, whose difficulty in managing adolescence and transitions I can now understand.

7 Bina: Observing cultural difference

For nine months I visited Bina, a young East African Asian girl, as my subject of observation. Bina lives with her mum and dad along with her paternal grand-parents and other members of her father's family at times, in particular his younger brother. Bina was 14 months old at the beginning of the period of observation, and almost two when it ended. During the period of observation, Bina's sister, Kanak, was born. The family live above the post office and general hardware store which they run, and which is located in an area with a fairly high proportion of Asian families. Other close relations, great aunt, aunts and uncles, and cousins, live in very close proximity to the family.

To find a young child to observe, I approached a health visitor I knew who was able to put me in touch with this family through one of her colleagues. I did not know her colleague, and I had no knowledge of this family whatsoever before the process of observation began.

I was particularly interested in observing a child in a family from a different ethnic and cultural origin to my own. I wanted the opportunity to think about a different culture and the influence of different patterns of family interaction, particularly on the mother/child relationship.

I, like others in the group, found it rather daunting to assume the mantle of an observer rather than of someone involved in active intervention. The balance between integration with and separation from the family seemed as complex at times for the observer as it was constantly for the developing child. Martha Harris (1987) points out that it is "... felt to be important that the observer should feel him/her self sufficiently inside the family to experience the emotional impact, but not committed to act out any roles thrust upon him/her, such as giving advice or registering approval or disapproval". Easier said than done! The withholding of advice when requested felt very uncomfortable at first until the role was more established, and the power of the emotional impact was easy to underestimate. Close observation of infant behaviour and response can be a very painful experience and it was important that we were able to think, within our seminar groups, about how some of our observations had made us feel and why.

Bina's mother is from Zambia and first came to England at 12, when she began attending boarding school here. Her parents are in business and seem to spend their lives between England and home in Zambia. She has older siblings, and a younger brother and sister are currently at school in England. During the period of observation her mother came to live in England for a period of time and mother, Bina and Kanak spent a lot of time with her. Mother often seemed to be crying out for mothering, and, after spending time with her own mother, she was certainly calmer and stronger, and seemed more able to make her own feelings and wishes known. Mother is attractive, intelligent and articulate but often seemed like the child herself, and had not resolved her dilemma about the conflict between a career and being a good mother. Her English was perfect and she talked of many

English friends, but most of her life was spent firmly enclosed within a Hindu culture, and within her husband's family.

Bina's father is from Kenya and he has been in the UK with his family for many years. He has a younger brother who is at university in England and lives with them during the holidays. He appeared to be a quiet, calm man, always working in the shop but with time during the day to spend with mum and Bina, whenever he could. He was the gatekeeper, always there when I arrived and when I left, putting a frame and a structure around my time spent there. Dad's dilemma was that he appeared to be the father to Bina and sometimes mother too, but he had the constant presence of his own parents in the home. It was never clear who owned the home or the shop but neither of his parents worked there. During the period of observation, dad bought a bungalow in a neighbouring town, but mum made it clear that her parents-in-law would move there with them.

My observations covered the period between early October and the following July, after an initial meeting in September to make a contract with mum and the family about my role as an observer and the purpose of it. It was difficult to maintain a really consistent pattern and structure to my visits as mum often had to change times and cancel visits because of illness or family arrangements. The birth of Kanak meant that I missed three weeks of observations and later in the year, mum, Bina and Kanak spent at least three weeks with grandmother and went on holiday with her. Looking back over the whole period of observation, it does feel as if it was disrupted quite often, and there were very few occasions when I was able to observe only mum and Bina together. I think that this clearly reflects the patterns of familial functioning and culture and has an important bearing on the contents of my observation.

This leads on, in a sense, to the specific feature of my observations to which I would like to draw closer attention: what I can only describe as the 'multiplicity' of Bina's carers. At the time of the observations, and since, I have tried to reflect on the significance of the fact that Bina had a large number of adult carers involved in her life and, more importantly, that she appeared to have more than one primary carer living with her and involved day to day in her care. I am in no real position to draw any definite conclusions from my observations. I merely share them in terms of behaviour which I saw and family patterns of which I was aware. Bina has three extremely important carers living with her; her mum, her dad, and her paternal grandmother. Though mum and dad speak extremely good English, her grandmother's English is limited. The family are Hindu and the language spoken at home is Gujerati. Over the period of my observations, while Bina's language was developing, her use of Gujerati far outweighed her use of English. Clues which others may have been able to hear in terms of verbal communication were not always accessible to me, so it was even more important to observe behaviour closely.

The first point to make is that, interestingly enough, I was not immediately aware of the fact that Bina's paternal grandparents lived with the family. Mum did not volunteer the information on first meeting, and it was only over a period of time that I became aware of this. For the first nine visits before Christmas, I was observing Bina during the afternoon, while grandmother was at work, and I never met her. On three or four occasions I was able to see only Bina and mum; however, very often, another relative would be there or would call in always during my visit. These were aunts, cousins, or mum's younger siblings.

During these early visits, a feature which recurred and which was often noted during our seminar discussions was that Bina was constantly picked up and put down somewhere and activity often seemed quite frenetic. Both mum and Bina seemed to have some inhibitions about prolonged physical holding which rarely took place. However, the only occasions when Bina seemed to be very content and happy were when mum was able to sit with her on her knee for any length of time and read to her or just hold her. I note:

On one visit mum arrived back in the room, picked up Bina and cuddled her on her knee, while Bina drank from her bottle. Bina was quiet and contented, snuggling into mum and she stayed there for several minutes. Bina got down. She did not want to, but mum put her down. She picked up and discarded a couple of toys then walked over to me to stare and cry.

I note:

Mum got the bottle from the shelf and picked Bina up. Bina lay back and snuggled in and held her bottle. Mother said that she did not normally do this; only when I was there, as she might usually be helping in the shop or taking Bina for a walk or to her aunt's house.

Bina was generally rather demanding and rarely contented. During these early weeks it was easy to see her as a young child very aware of the imminent arrival of a rival (new baby) as mum was quite heavily pregnant and talked freely about the baby who was due to be born. However, later, I was to wonder about the significance of the absent carers during these early weeks.

Typically, when I arrived, during the weeks before Christmas, mum would be in the downstairs kitchen, preparing food or coffee. Also typically, Bina would be put down on one of the kitchen worktops. I note:

We walked through, Bina still in mum's arms. When we reached the kitchen mum put Bina down on the working surface while she put water in the kettle. Again, I write "As usual, mum put Bina down on the working surface while she put coffee in the cups, but Bina was whiny and putting up her arms to be picked up."

On a much later occasion, when Bina acted jealously towards a cousin and took away a toy, I note:

Mum quickly came over and took the toy and gave it back to the little girl, smacking Bina and saying she must learn to share. Mum picked up Bina and put her on top of the back of the settee, telling her to sit there until she calmed down. Bina was sobbing and holding herself really rigidly - looking very precarious.

After Kanak had been born, and when grandmother was always present, I was able to observe the picking up, putting down and passing on pattern quite often. The care of the girls was very much shared and there was a great deal of passing on of one or other child from mum to grandmother, or vice-versa. I write:

Grandmother picked up Kanak, patting her back. Mum came back in carrying Bina who was wrapped in a big towel. Mum put Bina down and she began running over to her uncle who was in the room. Mum went over and took Kanak from her grandmother. Grandmother then grabbed Bina and began to rub her dry and try to dress her.

Bina often climbed up into her high chair or climbed into her basket, after emptying the toys, as if she felt secure there.

Another regular feature of Bina's behaviour was her enjoyment of dancing in circles, at times spinning until she collapsed on the floor. I write:

Bina listened to the music and made dancing movements. She giggled. She started walking and running round and round the toy and mum said she would get dizzy. Bina knocked the toy over and flopped on to the floor.

When I look back over my observations, there are few which do not contain a mention of Bina spinning or running in a circle, or playing ring-a-ring-a-roses. If there were several adults in the room, she would often run between them, touching each one and then passing on to the next.

In our seminar group we reflected, on several occasions, that Bina was a child who did not seem to feel very 'held'. She would run and spin and touch and go, would be picked up and put down, would sit on a lap then struggle down, shrug off a towel and run around the room, pat a leg and run away, and she rarely stayed to hold and explore and discover. Mum herself seemed at times to need holding and calming, and the level of change and movement and activity in the household was high. It was clear from my observations after Kanak had been born that it was grandmother who felt most confident about handling, managing, changing and dressing the children, and that mum was often de-skilled and put in the position of a child. I began to wonder about the difficulties of parenting confidently in such a situation, and also about the effect on Bina of having more than one primary carer. Studies have clearly shown that the strength of infant attachment is connected closely to maternal behaviour and, I believe, the confidence of the mother in respect of her handling of the child. Bina was not often readily comforted by handling and close bodily contact, except when only one important carer was involved and in the room, and I felt at times that she displayed an anxious attachment as opposed to a secure attachment to her mother, and at times her grandmother also. It may be that Bina found it very difficult to construct a clear hierarchy of attachment figures and that this led to confusion and bewilderment at times.

What do I know? All I can say is that quite often, Bina seemed to be spinning in a void without any one clear person to catch her, and to hold her, until she felt safe. Children often play games like this and my reactions might have been distortions of the observation process. As I said earlier, I cannot begin to justify most of what I have said or to draw firm conclusions. I am only able to present some observed behaviour and some tentative thoughts.

Standing outside the situation, I do not intend to criticize an extensive kinship network which taken as a whole provided secure emotional support for the children. The amount of material within the weekly observations is so vast that it leaves you gasping. This, too, makes me cautious in writing about my subjective reactions. It leads me on to the issue of how the learning from the observations applied specifically to social work training.

The overwhelming impact on me was of how much there is to see and learn, how long it takes and how slowly it happens. Also, how easy it is to interpret behaviour in any number of different ways. I began to feel de-skilled in my role of social worker in terms of making assessments. We constantly make assessments on such brief contact and tentative information and use these as the basis of ongoing work with clients. Hopefully, we are skilled enough to re-assess constantly and form different hypotheses in order to effect change. I feel very strongly now that as social workers, we must listen and learn from those workers like family centre workers, day centre workers and residential workers, who actually spend time day by day with clients and are able to observe behaviour and patterns of interaction over a period of time.

I consider that the period I spent observing Bina and her family was a privilege and a valuable learning experience, after a lot of years actively in social work tasks. To have the opportunity to observe and later in seminar groups to identify learning and evaluate experience, without intervening or holding the constraint of responsibility for protection or change, was a unique chance to learn and rediscover basic important skills.

It is clear to me now that observation has an extremely important part to play in social work education. The ability to see and learn about a child, or any client, as an individual in interaction with his/her important objects, is a valuable skill in understanding every aspect of development – social, physical, intellectual and emotional. It is a tool in assessments and in the process of decision making about child protection and 'good enough' parenting, as well as giving more confidence to social workers in direct work with children and communicating with children.

Part IV
Attachments and separations: normal life events

8 Ben: Depression or developmental delay?   73

9 Anthony: Responding to mother's return to work   80

10 David: The birth of his brother   88

Introduction

Through essays about Ben, Anthony and David, this part focuses on how aspects of modern life impact on childrens' normal developmental stages. The essays demonstrate how children, siblings, parents and carers adjust to painful but inevitable transitions.

Ben's development causes concern as his mother cares for him and older sister Kate single-handed during his father's prolonged absences. Anthony experiences change when his mother returns to work and nannies enter the household. David is observed preparing for and adjusting to the birth of his brother Michael.

The intensity of the observation process causes normal developmental tasks of attachments and separations to seem unbearably painful. Observers, however, receive distorted messages about the complexity of emotion involved in children's developmental stages and in particular the handling of attachments and separations. By focusing on the child rather than discussing issues with the adult carers, as social workers would do, the observer may present an overly pessimistic perspective on a normal life process. The obvious resilience and strength of Ben, Anthony and David serve to put things into perspective. These essays have relevance to those planning and providing day care for the under fives.

8 Ben: Depression or developmental delay?

Ben is the second child of Howard and Kate; he has one sister Anna, aged two. The family lives in the upstairs flat of an Edwardian terraced house, with kitchen, and living room and three bedrooms, all laid out on a long corridor; they also have the use of the back garden. I started to visit Ben when he was six weeks old.

I set up this observation through a personal contact; I asked a friend who has two children of the same age as Anna and Ben to ask in the playgroup for a possible child. I specified that I wanted to observe a young baby, and explained, that I was interested in the child's development over the first year of life. When I visited Kate to negotiate the observation she told me that her husband Howard would be away a lot in the summer and that she would welcome a visitor.

It also turned out that Kate and my friend and another mother from the playgroup became close friends and spent a good deal of time in each other's houses, particularly on playgroup mornings. I therefore entered a situation in which personal and professional boundaries were blurred and it was often difficult to hold to a defined role as an observer; I had to be careful to maintain confidentiality about what Kate said to me, and I tried to be clear about the focus of my visits.

My original interest in development became a theme of the observation, and clearly structured the way in which Kate and Howard viewed me. For a time this was also a major worry both for the parents and for myself. As I was involved in occasional care of a child who is a month older than Ben, I could make a comparison between the two children, and I also had some current involvement in the experience of looking after small children. Both of these were factors which I had anticipated as interesting and positive; in the event they proved to be difficult and painful.

Kate's isolation

Kate told me from the start that she was missing Howard. He was away from April to late August. Throughout the early months of the observation Kate complained little about this, beyond saying occasionally that she missed him, and more frequently that Anna missed her dad. While he was working away Howard came home very infrequently, and only for brief periods such as Saturday night and Sunday. Kate said that she could have gone to visit him but couldn't face the journey.

When he returned in September, they had a holiday with Kate's parents, and in October there was a period when Howard was at home by day and I saw him with Ben.

From September, when Howard returned, Kate complained more frequently about his absences, saying things like: "How would you know? You were never here." She also said how much easier it was, especially at night, to look after the two children, when there was another adult in the house. She looked back and said she could not think how she managed when Howard was away and Ben was small. Kate also began to complain about the fact that Howard never got up in the night to look after either Anna or Ben.

Anna's sleep patterns

Anna regularly woke at night and disturbed Kate. Because of this Kate was frequently very tired. I have often visited in the morning to find her white and drawn; she would then give me a blow by blow account of the night. When Howard was away, Kate said that she felt that Anna woke up at night because she missed her father; at this time Kate was also feeding Ben during the night and, as a result, got very little sleep. Finally, she asked advice from her health visitor, who set up a behavioural programme for Anna. For a time Kate was hopeful that this would help. Ben dropped night feeds by July, but Anna continued to wake with nightmares. Kate said that she took Anna into her bed as this was the only thing that seemed to work. Anna once told me that she was frightened of the ducks in her bed. I think that Kate felt that no-one took the night disturbance seriously enough. She said to me: "Perhaps you should sleep here, then you would see what it is like."

On reading the recordings again, I am struck by the constant recurrence of accounts of sleepless nights, and by the effect that this must have on Kate's wellbeing.

Kate's support network

Kate was supported by a network of female kin. The closest support was her sister Sarah. During May, June and July Sarah came in almost every day and acted as informal mother's help for Kate. During this period she took Anna out and did shopping and other tasks. Sarah was a lifeline. In August Sarah went to Spain and fell in love with a Spaniard. Kate recounted this with amusement and a touch of envy. The affair didn't last and Sarah was back but not in such close contact. When I met Sarah I felt that she offered not only practical help, but also companionship and liveliness.

Kate also received help from her mother, but her feelings about this were more ambivalent. Ben's grandmother came up once a week to look after the children while Kate went to her singing class. Kate paid weekend visits to her parents and in February, she left both children with her parents. Her mother would have offered more help but Kate would not accept this. Anna was said not to suffer from night terrors when she stayed with her granny, and one suggestion was that Anna should spend a longer time with her granny in the summer; Kate refused this. On this occasion Kate was clearly resentful of her family's concern and Sarah was acting as chief negotiator in a series of telephone calls. Kate also had a disabled sister who took part in riding for the disabled shows and competitions. Kate and the children often went to see her. Kate's grandmother was still alive and owned the caravan which the family borrowed in the summer; her mother and her grandmother were often not on speaking terms and Kate acted as mediator through letters and telephone calls.

Ben's social world: triadic interaction

From the first observation, when Ben was seven weeks old, Kate was making comparisons between the two children. My initial impression of Ben was of his size and Kate commented as she first showed him to me "He is a very big baby ... bigger than Anna." As well as being big he was said to sleep a lot. In the initial weeks it was difficult to find a time to visit because "... he sleeps a lot, he is much more contented than Anna, he sleeps a lot more ... she's the one who wakes at night."

Kate continued to describe Ben as contented. In an observation in January Kate says "he never cries, he is such a contented chap". Anna, by contrast, is described as never sitting still. In the first observation Kate is appreciative, in her description of Anna: "Anna is a constant interest, she does something new every day".

As the months passed Kate's descriptions of Anna's behaviour became more exasperated, and traits for which she had previously been praised, such as cleverness and quickness, were described in a more critical way. In October the response to screaming is, "she is getting even more impossible" and Anna is picked up by one arm and put outside the door. When she is described as bright this is followed by a belittling comment: "Anna is the bright one - little miss clever".

By January, when he was 10 months old, Ben was also defined in gender terms: "He is interested in cars, he is interested in boy's toys - quite different from Anna". At this time Kate was casting forward in her mind to imagine Ben as a small boy: "I can't imagine him in fights with other small boys, he is a softy despite his size". Kate also expected that she will have a different relationship with Ben because he is a boy "Mothers get very close to their sons".

On my last visit, when Ben was a year old, Kate commented that Ben and Anna got on very well: "They play really well together, it is her and me who fight".

This comment was made as Anna was picked up, kicking and screaming, and carried into her room to be dressed. On her return Anna was complaining about the clothes that her mother had chosen for her. These isolated comments about the children are picked out from a mass of communications between myself and Kate, but they seem to represent a shift in the relationship between Kate and Anna as gender roles in the family begin to be defined. It is also possible to hypothesize that a pattern of ambivalent closeness between mother and daughter is being established for the third generation.

By the time Ben was a year old he and Anna could be described by Kate as playing together, but there had been interaction between Ben and Anna from the first observation. When Ben was seven weeks Kate encouraged Anna to kiss Ben. Anna wanted to hold him and Kate sat her down on the floor with the baby on her knees. The pattern of stroking and kissing continued, but Anna became rougher in her kisses. In November she grabbed him from behind and kissed and licked him and almost bit him. A week later she hugged and squeezed him so that he cried. On the few occasions that I have heard Ben cry it has been when Anna has pushed him over. Once he learned to crawl he began to take pieces of Anna's puzzle and Kate commented that "he can annoy his sister now".

He could also co-operate more with his sister. In January he could take shapes from her and post them. In March they were crawling after each other around table legs.

At three months Ben was following Anna with his gaze, and from this moment until he learned to crawl at ten months old his gaze was frequently fixed on Anna and any other small children. He followed the movements of the children more frequently than his mother. From the first observation Kate was encouraging Anna to wave a rattle for Ben, and Anna continued to give him toys. There was often a sense of frustration as he did not take the toys which she offered. Once he was crawling, Anna came and sat close to him and Kate moved her, telling her not to crowd him.

Throughout the visits Kate used me to occupy one of the children while she attended to the other. On the first visit she gave me Ben while she cuddled Anna who was upset at the sight of a stranger. Once she became accustomed to me, Anna wanted attention. As her talk became more lively she talked constantly and asked questions. I often played with Ben while Kate did something with Anna. Although I had begun the observation by thinking I should concentrate exclusively on Ben, I came to see Ben's early experience as necessarily including Anna, and the sibling interaction as vitally important (Dunn and Kendrick 1982). I also realized the truth of Kate's complaint that child care is much easier with more than one pair of hands.

Interaction between mother and infant

The most intimate moments that I observed between Ben and Kate were when she was changing him on his changing mat in the bathroom. For example, at three months:

She kisses him and strokes his hair and talks to him and he vocalizes back ... She calls him a big boy and her big boy and again kisses and strokes him as he lies on his mat; she says he likes looking at the movement of the towels.

Later, in October and November, Kate would sing to Ben while she changed him.

By contrast the times when I saw Ben breast feeding I did not see much interaction. In the first few observations Ben was put to the breast in response to crying. At four months he was given a bottle of juice, but Kate continued to breast feed him until he was nine months old. The last time I saw him take the breast was at nine months and he was wriggling and refusing the nipple. In the early feeds he sucked steadily while Kate gave her attention to something else. She told me that she did not believe in burping babies, so Ben was often put down immediately after his feed. From July he started to eat solids and by November he was eating steadily from a spoon, but Kate was not giving him the spoon to feed himself when he tried to take it because he made such a mess. By February he was using the spoon himself.

From the age of three months Ben was placed on the floor to kick and offered rattles or balls to play with; he was also put in a baby chair with toys on strings to look at. He was encouraged to use his hands and to listen to sounds. Once he was sitting on his own, he sat surrounded by toys, but paid very little attention to them.

In my first observation Kate put Ben down out of earshot when he started to cry, saying she would put him somewhere where she could not hear him. The look that accompanied this remark seemed to defy me to comment. The next week Kate said that she had found he wouldn't cry himself to sleep! In fact Ben cried very little during the mornings while I was visiting and as soon as he started to grizzle Kate tended to put him down to rest.

Concern about Ben's development

I had a sense from the beginning that Ben was a very passive child. I was also surprised to find that I did not like him; he didn't evoke in me the usual adult response of wanting to smile and talk to babies. The gradual build up of depression in me was such that I failed to return after the summer holidays and there is a gap of two and a half months in my visits.

The first visit which I made in October was very disturbing; Ben did not appear to be developing in the way which I would expect for a baby of seven months. I now think that I didn't pay sufficient attention to the fact that Ben had just recovered from an attack of croup and that Kate had again been up all night, but the picture was still worrying.

Ben was sitting on the floor surrounded by toys but taking no interest in them. He didn't put the toys in his mouth or reach for them, he didn't respond when Anna built a tower out of beakers and knocked it over; when Anna pushed him over he didn't cry or protest. He followed Anna with his gaze, but didn't react to me as a stranger or notice his mother leaving the room. Later in the observation Kate sat at the kitchen table with Ben on her lap and he sat still without reaching for her cup or trying to get her attention in any way. She left him on the table while she tended Anna and he didn't wriggle off.

In response to the seminar discussion after this visit I charted Ben's developmental capacities over five visits. The picture wasn't as worrying as I had thought. Ben did laugh and smile at Kate when he was being changed, he touched Kate's face and spoke when he was being fed with the spoon and he shouted when feeding stopped. He occasionally smiled at me. He picked up toys and responded to musical toys with a shout. He waved his hands and legs excitedly and pushed himself gradually round on the floor. Kate was beginning to pick up his vocal sounds and give them meaning as words "mummy" or "hallo".

Parental fears

But I was not the only person who had been worried about Ben's development. Kate used my visits as means of reassurance:

"You'll notice a great difference in him" (October).

"He has got some new tricks to show you" (November).

"It is quite usual not to crawl at eight months" (November).

Sometimes she was more direct in her worries, as when she told me that I needn't bother to close the stair gate "you needn't bother, he's not crawling yet" and when he began to play with his post box "He's quite clever, I thought he wasn't going to be up to much".

When I first met Howard in October he was even more direct "you picked a duff one here, he doesn't develop - only gets bigger". I was chilled by this comment, and didn't know how to answer. On the three occasions that I saw Howard with Ben I was struck that he picked him up and took him round the kitchen on one hip and also held him up in the air and tickled him. Once he had returned, Howard got the children up in the morning and gave them breakfast. Kate welcomed the chance of some sleep, but was mildly critical of what the children were given to eat and of Howard's choice of clothes.

'He's crawling!'

I was greeted in late January when Ben was 10 months old with this cry of triumph and relief "you missed it by a few hours, he's crawling". There was equal relief in my recording

It's true – he does crawl. ..Ben sees the cat behind the chair and goes to investigate, giving a shout. The cat retreats and I say that cats are more interesting than toys. Kate says, so is the fireplace and the coal and the tongs (I have a real sense of release that Ben has at last escaped from the surrounding circle of plastic toys).

From this moment Ben was more active. He imitated adults and took toys from Anna, he wriggled to get off his mother's lap. He tried to pull himself up on the edge of the settee. He crawled after Kate and then paused and investigated the coal scuttle and looked at me, before turning and crawling into the kitchen. The following week he smiled at me and felt my cord trousers. He crawled into a pile of bottles in the kitchen and was rescued by Kate. His vocal range was extending, and he both shouted and cried more than he did. At last, after so many months, I began to like him and to respond by laughing and touching him. There was an easier feel about the visits. When I visited with a present in March I was relieved that Ben cried when I approached him and that he and Anna fought over the present.

Conclusion

I am still uncertain about the reasons for Ben's slow development. Was this a response to Kate's depression in the early months, or simply his innate temperament? In so far as his passivity was a response to her depression one could suggest that he became more active as Kate became less isolated and more able to express some of her frustrations with Howard. I am also uncertain how far the judgement of slow development was arrived at because of the middle-class expectations of both parents and observer. Thinking about possible applications to social work assessment, I am sure that an assessment cannot be made on the basis of one visit. My view of Ben on the October visit was certainly skewed by my own anxiety and I also failed to take sufficient account of the child's recent illness. Finally, I have been depressed by the social isolation and the process of gender construction which I have observed in this family. I feel that this reflects the social position of women and I would hope that the detail of child observation can be set in a wider context as described by Hanmer and Statham (1988):

"Truly to understand the experience of mothers and mothering is to look beyond the mother-child relationship to the social forces and policies that shape and restrain its expression. Looked at in this way, the experience of becoming a mother and caring for children is not inevitable, biologically dictated, or a private matter unconnected to the rest of society, but the result of social organisation ... That which is socially organised can be altered" (page 54).

9 Anthony: responding to mother's return to work

Anthony was born to Jane and Peter. He is Jane's first child; Peter has two daughters by his first marriage. They live with their mother outside London but spend alternate weekends with Jane and Peter. The family lives in a comfortable three-bedroom house and Anthony has his own room.

Jane is a high achieving professional in her thirties. She told me at our first meeting that she was planning to go back to work after six months, and that this would mean returning full-time as part-time work was not possible.

Peter is also a professional. He changed jobs during the latter period of my observation, and so spent a few weeks at home once Jane had gone back to work. Both parents appear to be hard-working 'high-achievers'.

A full-time, live-out nanny was employed, beginning the week before Jane returned to work. A temporary appointment for three months was followed by another nanny for Anthony.

Due to some delays in setting up the observation, I did not visit for the first time until Anthony was 11 weeks old. I regret missing this crucial early period, and my knowledge of his very early life is solely from Jane's reports.

Themes

Jane's return to work was something of a crisis for the family. I have the impression that she has always been a 'success' in her life, and needed things to be perfect in her new role as mother. When things were going well, in the early days of my visit, they seemed almost idyllic. Once she was not going to be a constant presence for Anthony she seemed to need this to be fine too, rather than accepting that it would be painful for a time. I seem to have been prevented for a time from seeing anything but the lovely bits, and there was no space for Anthony to express his pain either. He became ill with a series of increasingly severe chest infections, and I assume that as there was no other outlet capable of holding his feelings, he was forced to vent his distress somatically.

The observation

The first three times I visited Anthony and Jane, in the late afternoon, most of the hour was taken up with breast feeding, which both seemed to really enjoy.

On my first visit he lay still in her arms and gazed at her intently while he fed: she frequently looked down at him and smiled. I had almost the sense of intruding on a very intense relationship, that they were both very wrapped up in each other. Once Jane looked up at me and commented: "He rolls off and grins at me sometimes – it's so sweet".

He stopped sucking briefly and she put her arms across his back and lifted him to the breast again and he resumed. His right hand occasionally moved slightly, up and down, and once both his arms flailed so she shifted position on the sofa, leaning forwards slightly to see if that made him more comfortable, and he became still again.

In my next two visits I noted at the time that Jane seemed well attuned to Anthony's feelings and needs. She knew if he was tired or off colour by his gestures before he cried. On my third visit we were in Anthony's bedroom where he was about to be undressed for his bath, and she switched on a new musical box above his head hoping that it would distract him while she ran the bath. When he heard this new noise he laughed with absolute delight and reached out to it. She bent down and laughed with him, seeming equally delighted by his delight and it seemed a perfect example of that instinctive "reflecting back of an infant's feeling state" which Stern (1985, page 144) says is so important to the infant's developing knowledge of his or her own affectivity and sense of self.

All my notes from this time seem relentlessly positive, as I look back on them, and I suspect that I was seduced by the perfect picture Jane seemed to hold in her mind.

On my fifth visit, when Anthony was nearly four months old, he had started to sleep through the night, and was beginning to take some solid food. Jane had been to a work function that lunchtime and her colleagues had made a big fuss over Anthony. He was noticing me and smiling at me a lot that day; Jane had laid him on the carpet near his activity centre while she went to make some tea but he spent the time beaming at me. When she came back into the room she began speaking to him, about his tooth but he continued to smile at me while I smiled back. Jane commented: "You'd rather look at Mary than boring old mummy you see every day, wouldn't you?" This had been Jane's first foray back into her world of work and I wondered if Anthony had sensed this new call on her attention and was getting his own back by paying more attention to me than usual.

When I visited the following week and she laid him on the bed to change him, I again had a sense of rivalry between myself and Jane for Anthony's attention. He had been quiet and seemed sleepy when she carried him upstairs.

As he lay down and she removed his nappy he noticed me looking at him and began to smile at me. Jane spoke to him, commenting affectionately on the contents of his messy nappy, but he did not divert his gaze from mine. Jane began to rotate his legs quite energetically and saying "you're riding a bike, Anthony". This caused him to refocus on her and she beamed at him and scooped him up. He then nestled sleepily into her neck.

I had the sense that I had overstepped the mark from being an observer to being a participant in Anthony's life, and began to wonder whether I ought not to return his smiles. Peter was at home this day and, a few minutes later, when Anthony began to cry slightly after sitting peaceably on Jane's lap, he suggested that Anthony might be hungry. Jane replied that she'd been trying to give him the breast but it felt as if he was rejecting her. Peter replied that he'd meant solid food and he took Anthony from her and went into the kitchen in search of a jar of food. Jane's tone had been humorous, but her use of the word 'rejected' indicated to me that she was finding any sign of Anthony's individuation from her – inevitable as he grew and formed relationships with others, and took nourishment from outside of her body – to be painful, and perhaps an interruption of their joint paradise. It might also be that as her work life had begun to encroach and she became conscious of an approaching need to separate from him, there was an underlying sense of guilt about whether she was causing the change or pushing him away.

I ought to say that as I read my notes I am conscious that I seem to have paid at least as much attention to what was going on for Jane as for Anthony. Often the room was filled with her thoughts and feelings and I could not find space to think specifically about Anthony. The overbearing nature of her feelings became more noticeable later when the need not to see his or her own pain meant that attention was not paid to Anthony's experiences by either parent. I only saw Peter rarely during my early visits, but I speculate that these distractions from attending to Anthony, which on occasion affected me, also affected him.

When I visited again after Christmas Anthony was said to be teething and sleeping very badly. She often had to get up to him in the night and so Jane and Anthony often ended up sleeping in the spare room together. He was also breast feeding much less; Jane told me that it was 'not enough for him now' and also it hurt her now he had teeth. The breast-feeding relationship was obviously not a lovely experience for either of them any more.

Until now Peter's role had been rather passive as far as I could observe. He got home around seven in the evening and when I was there to observe, came in and pecked Anthony on the cheek before going up to change. Jane would then inform him about key aspects of Anthony's and her day while he played with Anthony for a short while before bed. On my third visit to the family he had commented to me, when he came home and found me watching Anthony asleep: "They're boring to observe now, aren't they?". He told me that Anthony liked 'rough play', and on my fifth visit I saw him move Anthony around in the air in a prone position quite fast saying: "You're a helicopter!" while Anthony squealed delightedly. He then held him quietly against his shoulder while both got their breath back before placing him on the floor and ruffling his hair. I gather that this is classic paternal behaviour. Brazelten and Cramer (1990, page 106) talk about the qualitative differences between mother-infant and father-infant interaction, and say that '... fathers are more likely to play heightened, stimulating games. They poke and touch, heightening the baby's state of excitement ... a rhythm of higher peaks and longer periods of recovery characterizes infants' interactions with their fathers in contrast to their mother.' One could speculate that the 'rough play' concealed some hostility to the new male in the house who was absorbing most of his wife's attention, but in the brief periods in which I saw Peter at this time I didn't have this sense.

From early January, Peter's role appeared to me to be more prominent – there was less deference to Jane as the 'Anthony expert' for example. From the time when the child moves away from breast-feeding the father (or anyone else outside the mother-infant dyad) becomes capable of playing a larger part in his care of course. During the same time Jane was asked and agreed to return to work a bit earlier than she had planned. In one sense this would put both parents on the same footing, out of the house all day and delegating Anthony's care to another adult. On my seventh visit Anthony had an ear infection, and on Peter's return from work he held him on his knee and examined the ear, and spoke authoritatively about Anthony needing to be bathed "only on his lower half" in a tone I had not heard before. Jane listened apparently compliantly. Later in the same visit, Jane was feeding Anthony from a jar of something fish-flavoured, and Peter commented: "I don't remember trying to feed fish to the girls when they were babies". I was reminded that this was not Peter's first involvement with child-rearing, as it was for Jane, and it was as if she was relegated to the less experienced one. I could not see her face as she crouched beside Anthony with her back to me, but that was the sense I carried away with me.

At the same time Anthony was becoming a little more physically independent. I noted on my eighth visit, when he was four months old, that he was beginning to roll over by himself and so was more mobile about the floor, able to reach out and grab things. He was always interested in me when I came, too. In general he was clearly interacting with his environment much more actively as he grew.

These factors seemed to conspire to make Jane question her 'special relationship' with Anthony just when work was claiming her more and more. She had several phone calls and invitations to give lectures at work preparatory to her comeback. When I visited at the end of January she was looking quite stressed. Anthony, she said, was "grizzling" a lot – they had had a busy day with lots of people around and he had not been able to sleep. She was trying to get on with clearing up but he wanted to be held and he cried whenever she put him down.

Eventually she put him to her breast tiredly, and he stopped crying and started to suck immediately. She said: "Oh Anthony you'll have to get used to managing without this comforter soon". Then the phone rang and she had to disturb him to answer it, saying: "I'm sorry, I'm sorry, I should have brought the phone in here". He lay on the sofa quietly while she ran into the other room fetched the phone, and came back. It was a work colleague and she talked into the telephone, crooking the receiver into her neck while she held Anthony on her lap. She carried on the conversation, which seemed quite technical, while occasionally making faces at Anthony to distract him. He stood on her lap with her free arm around his waist, gazing at her. After a minute she lowered him onto the floor and slipped his dungarees off, ready to change his nappy. She was giving some advice over the phone, and at one point asked for some paperwork to be brought round to her over the weekend. Anthony lay passively on his back for a minute and kicked his legs about. She undid his nappy with one hand and found it was very dirty. She did not have the materials to hand to change him, and so she held both of his ankles with one hand and raised him above the nappy. She smiled down at him and jiggled his ankles from side to side, while still concentrating on her phone conversation. He smiled back at her at first, then stopped smiling. After about two minutes of stillness he turned himself on his side slightly and she let go the ankles. He curled up with his toes nearly touching his face, just away from the soiled part of the nappy. He remained in that position for another minute or so and then he started to cry. Jane leant down and stroked his back but, when he continued to cry, told her caller she'd have to ring back. She ran off to collect the changing things, and on her return I said that had been a very graphic demonstration of the juggling of two roles. She smiled ruefully. She changed Anthony swiftly and then raised him to her stomach and then above her. He smiled at her but not broadly.

This scene made a great impression on me; the presentiment that Jane was beginning to be more removed from Anthony and the guilt and pain that caused her, and Anthony's puzzlement at the change he did not understand, was vivid. On my next visit his ear infection had returned and he was poorly and fractious. Jane was struggling to manage him and seemed tired. He had to have some medicine in a syringe in his ears and she found it hard to administer – she commented that Peter managed it much better than she did and he'd give the next dose when he came home. Later, when Anthony grinned at me, she said "He's a showman. He's been grizzling all day and he's smiling now you're here. I had to take him into work yesterday and he was lovely with everyone, but when we came away he started crying again." She later said that for the last few days he hadn't wanted solid foods, only her milk, but she 'didn't know if she could produce enough any more.' It was as if she was moving away as fast as she could from their special relationship, stressing that others could do better with him, as if denigrating his need of her made her guilt easier to bear. Her distress seemed to prevent her from thinking about whether Anthony too was having a bad time. Rather, it was as if his needs and difficulties were persecuting her.

Anthony seemed to have a mix of different feelings as he coped with this new situation. In February, the week before Jane went back to work, Anthony had started accepting milk from the bottle. When I was there she was trying to feed him some solids but he kept turning his head away.

When she took him out of the high chair and sat him on her lap, he began clutching at her jumper by the breast. She thought from this that he wanted a breast feed and she offered him her nipple, but he refused to take it. She sat and just cuddled him for a while. He seemed to enjoy this, leaning his head against her neck, but then stiffened and noisily filled his nappy. Jane turned to me and suggested that he probably hadn't wanted to feed because he had been needing to do all that.

I am wondering as I write if she felt the need to offer this physical explanation in case I, as observer, might have felt there was some aggression in Anthony's act. I don't know whether she had felt it in this way but I know that I felt rather uncomfortable at the time.

On my next visit the nanny-to-be was present; she was shadowing Jane for the week before Jane went back to work. Anthony was grinning a lot, and was described by both women as a 'flirt' and a 'charmer'. He also smiled a lot at me. Nanny had made the tea – a carrot puree – and Jane commented that she was 'showing her up' by not using shop-bought food. Anthony was said to have been restless all day. Nanny fed him and he stared meanwhile at Jane who sat nearby and smiled at him. Later Jane played with Anthony, romping on the floor and he clutched at her, several times putting his mouth around her chin while she squealed and laughed. It must have been hard for him to understand why she was there and yet someone else was feeding him and taking the lead in bathing him, and feeding him, but he showed no obvious distress.

He seemed to exert himself to attract Nanny, who described him to me as 'gorgeous'. In fact I noticed increasingly in the coming months that he deployed his charm to ensure he got attention and affection wherever he was. He was a very attractive child physically, with tousled brown hair and large blue eyes, and I know that I felt increasingly attached to him as he made regular bids for my attention.

I visited two days after Jane had returned to work, when Anthony was almost exactly six months old. Peter was at home too, and both told me that everything was going well. Anthony 'loved' Nanny who played with him 'better than she (Jane) had ever done', and she'd slotted right back into work. Anthony was lying on her bed gurgling and smiling while she changed out of her work clothes. His cheeks were flushed and he smiled relentlessly throughout my visit. Jane sat on the bed and talked to him about his day and her day while he gurgled at her, and then Peter came in, sat down and began to tickle him. Jane said she was relieved that it had all gone so smoothly and he didn't seem to have suffered. This became a familiar pattern over the next two months; both Jane and Peter reported that things were going well, and Anthony seemed cheerful and contented, with no disturbances in his sleep or eating behaviour, although he had to adjust not only to Jane's absence but a change of routine to fit in with Nanny's style of caring; for example, she did not believe in feeding on demand, but in fixed mealtimes.

The next week I arrived just before Jane came home. Anthony was unwell with a cough, and had been quite clingy to Nanny.

Anthony was sitting on the rug near his box of toys. He was holding himself upright and clutching a soft toy when there was the sound of a key in the lock and Jane and Peter came in. Anthony had his back to the door and didn't turn round when she said: "Hi". She came over and sat by the rug. She leant over and touched his cheek, and then he turned and smiled at last.

His initial failure to respond to her reminded me powerfully of the 'still-face studies' which demonstrate the impact on a baby of a failure to achieve the expected attentive response from his mother. Bearing in mind that for some weeks Anthony had experienced his mother withdrawing emotionally from him before she withdrew physically, the comparison seems appropriate (Brazelton and Cramer 1991).

The following week I was there at the same time and when Jane came in she said to Peter: "Let's see if I get more of a reaction this time". I assume from this that she was regularly getting little response from Anthony at this time. That day, Nanny told me that Anthony had been sleeping an awful lot for the last two days, which may have been because he was becoming ill again, or it may have been another way of warding off his environment.

On my next visit I discovered a very sick child. His parents had called the emergency doctor after he began to have breathing difficulties. He was on antibiotics and Jane stayed home with him.

The following week he was said to have made a full recovery, although Jane said he wanted to be held by her all the time she was with him, or he cried. Just as I was leaving she asked me if it had occurred to me that there had been a lot of changes in Anthony's world, and perhaps that was why he had been ill. However, immediately she had spoken she added 'but no – he was really happy the first two weeks'. The following week, Anthony was unwell again.

I think it was this apparent inability or unwillingness to connect with the idea that Anthony was having a hard time without her that made these weeks so hard for them all. As Miller *et al.* (1991) observe in an ideal situation "a mother's capacities allow her not simply to register the baby's distress but to think about it (consciously or unconsciously) and respond in a thoughtful way. This means that she is in a position to modify the demands made on the baby's psyche by distressing experiences and at the same time give the baby his first contact with the human capacity for bearing pain through thinking" (page 26). Unfortunately Jane was not able to act as a container for the distress which he could not tolerate, and the stress took it's toll on the body instead. I would say that she could not bear to tune into his hatred of her for leaving him, and he received the message that he could not be angry with her, but his rage did not therefore vanish.

It is well recognized that internal disturbance can cause – or worsen – physical illness, although I do not deny that Anthony contracted an identifiable virus. Lewis (1991) observes that "Physical symptoms have been called a form of body language ... Since children, by virtue of their developmental stage, have concrete thinking and limited vocabulary, physical symptoms may well be used to communicate distress ... Similarly, families in which expression of emotions is discouraged may inadvertently foster the development of physical symptoms ... An anxious or depressed child may have little choice but to develop a somatic complaint or disabling symptom to express his or her misery" (page 701). In Anthony's case, I may add that there was also the 'secondary gain' of Jane's increased presence when he was ill.

After Anthony's second spell of illness I did not see Jane for my next five visits. On two occasions she was working late, on another two she went out straight from work, and the fifth she was expected 'any minute' but had not arrived by the time I left. I can only assume that, as she knew my task was to think about Anthony, from my observations, seeing me might have made her reflect on her son's experience in a way she did not want. This made me very uncomfortable, as I felt that I was perhaps carrying the bad parts of their recent history for them, and perhaps she was connecting me in her mind with this.

Anthony continued to grow and develop in spite of all the trauma. He learned to raise himself on his hands and legs, and then to stand while leaning against something. He had never been interested in crawling but he began to move about the room holding onto pieces of furniture. In early May Peter was at home more; the nanny still came and took practical care of Anthony while Peter played with him a lot. He was proud of Anthony's progress and never failed to point out another tooth, or another manoeuvre accomplished, and I was invited to admire uncritically. He did once speak about how 'horrible' it had been when Anthony was ill, how frightened he and Jane were – but added that Anthony had quite a good time charming the doctor and health visitor.

Peter seemed to regard himself as a junior partner to the new nanny, Mary, a brisk young woman. One day, when she had given Anthony his tea and then gone home, Peter remarked that she was a vegetarian and was not very 'tuned in' to giving Anthony meat. He said he was tempted to feed him some lamb casserole now she had gone (and smiled wickedly) but he decided he ought not to 'interfere'.

He romped a lot with Anthony, as he had always done, and Anthony responded. He told me in an amused tone that Anthony had taken to 'violent' splashing in the bath. On a visit in late May he showed me a toy he'd just bought Anthony, a hammer and pegs set. He kept encouraging Anthony to bash the pegs through their holes, but Anthony only wanted to suck the hammer. Peter was not inclined to analyse it when Anthony displayed any aggression; he saw him as a 'typical boy'.

For Anthony, Mary was another new face with another new routine – for example she preferred to bath him in the mornings. On my second visit after she was installed I noticed that he took little notice when she left but on the visit after that it was apparent that he kept her in sight for most of the time while she was preparing his food, and afterwards, craning his neck if necessary.

I next saw Jane and Anthony together at the start of June. When I arrived she was sitting and stroking his hair and telling him she had missed him, while he sat in his highchair. Mary appeared to be in charge – she asked Jane if she had put Anthony's eyedrops (for conjunctivitis) in 'properly' at the weekend, as his eyes now seemed worse. Jane asked for advice about how Mary did it.

On my next visit I was there before Jane. When she came in Anthony was passive at first, and then began to move back and forwards in his highchair excitedly. Jane said 'can I have a cuddle, or are you too independent now?' She got him out of his chair and threw him in the air, and he laughed. This was very much in Peter's style. As I write it seemed to me as if perhaps he had two fathers rather than a father and mother. Later Peter came in and wheeled Anthony round while Jane tickled him, and Anthony laughed a lot. Jane said he was 'daddy's boy'.

Conclusion

This was an uncomfortable observation in many ways, and the discomfort that Anthony must have experienced became more apparent to me in the writing of this paper than it had been at the time. The process, detailed earlier, which blunted my awareness of the feelings around me also stopped Anthony from identifying his pain, and this makes me feel, in retrospect, that I was identified with Anthony at the time; so that Jane prevented both of us from being in touch with our feelings.

By the time my observation ended the family seemed to have reached a tacit accommodation. Jane relinquished her special role as Anthony's mother while remaining a consistent, loving presence. I feel sad for Anthony; the network of care he now receives is certainly good enough but he used to have more. At the same time, he seems to be a survivor and is developing strategies for coping, such as bewitching those around him. I hope he carries on fighting for what he wants in the future.

10 David: The birth of his brother

My starting point is my feelings about being an observer. I found it hard to understand that a family would welcome a person into their home weekly for a year. However, in this instance it quickly became apparent that I had a very definite role. I was a weekly visitor for a limited time who did not make comments, criticisms or suggestions about what mum should be doing. I listened to what was being said without questioning or specific comments, which I must admit took a lot of getting used to. The ability to do this and feel comfortable has been a very worthwhile part of the experience of observation.

At this point I need to give a brief background of the family I observed. Mum is Julie 19 years old, Dad is Stuart, 24, and there was David who was six months old. The parents had been barely married a year when I first went. David was born in hospital and was four weeks premature. Julie had to spend six weeks in hospital before the birth as the consultant was concerned about the growth of the baby. Eventually Julie was induced and after over eight hours in labour, the latter part under epidural, David was born weighing six pounds. Up to David's birth the couple had lived with Julie's parents. The local council then provided a house which members of the family decorated and furnished before Julie and David came home. The home is a two bedroom council property with a large garden at back and front. It is on the outskirts of the town but on a good bus route. It was very basically furnished but during the year it has become much more cosy and comfortable.

Julie had worked with children before David's birth and had done a short child care course which she had enjoyed. Stuart worked in a local factory starting work at eight in the morning. Both parents and grandparents lived close by, and were in weekly contact.

My observations began when David was six months old. He was a bright, alert baby with blonde hair and large blue eyes. By then he weighed 16 pounds and was having three meals a day. Julie took him to the baby clinic every fortnight to keep a check on his weight. He used a baby walker to move around a little. He was able to sit up with the support of cushions.

After four observations Julie told me that she was pregnant again. The pregnancy was not planned and she did not feel ready for another baby. The temptation at this stage to be something other than an observer was great as Julie struggled to come to terms with the fact of her unplanned pregnancy. She was not ready emotionally to take on the demands of another baby. She had been enjoying David so much and felt this relationship would inevitably change. Julie and David did a lot of work together over the next months to prepare for the new baby. With the help of the seminar group I was able to keep strictly to my role as observer.

At times the observations were very painful as I saw a very relaxed, easy going situation change quite dramatically and quickly. There had never been pressure on David, but Julie began to demand and encourage him to do things which he was not physically ready to do. I observed this process on a number of occasions. For example, Julie bought David a new bottle with a hand grip which he could manage himself. At first he refused to use it.

Julie spent a lot of time encouraging him to crawl and insisted he walk as he moved from place to place. She would assist him with one hand and as he could barely sit up unaided, he was very wobbly for a long time. Julie also encouraged David to assist her when getting him dressed, e.g. lifting up his legs to get his trousers on, and giving her the correct foot to put his socks and shoes on. David responded to these requests and, although very difficult for him at times, he would nearly always make the effort.

This preparation for change began very early because Julie had the constant fear that she might be admitted to hospital for bed rest. Emotionally there was a distancing too. From there being lots of physical contact there were fewer cuddles unless Julie forgot herself and became engrossed in David. Prior to being an observer I had not fully understood the effect on the first child of the birth of a sibling. I want to look in some detail at David's perception of his mum's pregnancy and to come to a conclusion about the things he was able to understand.

David was eight months old when Julie knew she was pregnant again and she obviously began to worry about the pregnancy and impending birth. What would it mean to David, her family and for herself? David was then able to distinguish facial expressions and be aware of the difference in his mum's face. Gone was the smiling, alert attentive face to one which looked thoughtful, distracted and at times quite harassed.

Julie's shape changed and although this was gradual she began to stop the rough and tumble they used to have and was more careful when David was climbing on her. After a while David did not go to her to be picked up, but followed her around instead. This made me feel that he had understood and had been able to adapt to this distancing from his mum over a period of time.

Previously David had noticed my coming and going but never included me in play or asked me to do anything with him. David began to include me more, initially by conversing in his way. By this time Julie was eight months pregnant and had a very definite bump.

The conversations, although mostly babbling, had very definite intonations and he conversed in this way including both of us. Julie found this very trying because he never seemed to be satisfied with the response. (David by now was 13 months old.) The feeling I had was that David was looking for answers about the baby who was about to arrive. There was some talk about the baby but it was always indirect. There was very little preparation in a material sense until two weeks before.

I felt as if something awful was about to happen which David would definitely not like. I'm sure David could sense some of this as well.

Around this time my handbag became a fascination to him. It was as if he expected the baby to be produced out of it. He also compared my handbag to a seaside bucket. He looked in both several times and obviously expected to find something in either one.

David also played a lot in a large wooden toy box from which he was able to get in and out. He would empty a lot of the toys out and sit inside. Then he would get out but became tearful until he was helped to get back inside again. This made me wonder whether he was in some way remembering his own birth. He has continued to do this occasionally since the birth of the baby. David also started to look inside cupboards in the kitchen and living room and inside the baby box. There was a definite search for the baby or the change that was about to happen. Since the baby's birth David did the same searching when the baby was put to bed at night. He was not satisfied until he was taken to see him upstairs in bed.

As Julie's shape changed there was not as much room on her knee for him and the physical closeness they could have was distanced by the baby. When Julie carried David around there was also an obvious distance there which David would be aware of. He was clearly frustrated at times when he climbed up on Julie's knee. It felt like he was already having to share his mum.

Although I did not meet Stuart until much later, there was a definite move to involve him more in the care of David. It felt like a reluctant handing over of David by Julie to allow her space for the baby. From the conversations with Julie, Stuart appeared to be playing quite a lot with David. There were changes in the physical care and also in the emotional care. There was permission, albeit reluctant, to allow Stuart to have more involvement with David. Also it felt as if David was being pressurized to move from baby to toddler.

There were more conversations about Daddy and what he would do with David when he came home from work; play football, go to the park, work in the garden. David began to mention him more and after a holiday or weekend would look for him. It was Stuart who began to get up to David in the night if he woke up and get into bed with him if necessary. David seemed to adjust to this change. For Julie it seemed to be much more difficult.

At times Julie seemed depressed and preoccupied. David also looked very sad and dejected on these occasions, but would occupy himself in play. He did a lot of bashing of toys with his hands and his feet. At these times he would play for longish periods without demanding anything from his mum. It was only when he got frustrated or bored that he objected and then he would be offered the distraction or stimulation that he needed. However, I felt he had learned at this stage that his mum would not be able to give what she had previously. He had to try, therefore, to do what he could for himself. It felt as if David was confident enough to struggle by himself for a while, but the expectation was that Julie would be there if he found it too difficult. She always responded even though he may have had to wait a little while.

Julie began to involve David in more adult things, like putting things in the washing machine, or sorting out the washing after it had been dried There were constant conversations about what she was doing and what needed to be done next. David was always eager to help and was able to allow Julie to be out of the room if he knew what she was doing, because they had talked about it.

There was never any direct reference to the baby in the observations but indirect references, through adverts on television showing babies, or visits by people with babies. On these occasions David responded in a negative way. There was always an underlying anxiety about if he was going to like the baby.

As the time drew close for the baby's birth there was a definite feeling around Julie not being ready. David was very quiet and flat as well. He began to come to me more to look at books and to keep toys while he wanted them. However, I began to feel sure that David would be alright as he seemed to have made great strides physically and emotionally over the previous six months. At this stage there was support also from dad, grandparents and extended family.

I have been fortunate enough to be able to carry on observing after the birth of the baby Michael, when David was 17 months old. It has been very interesting to observe both babies and to test out the things I thought David had perceived. Julie was relieved that Michael was not so demanding as David had been when he was a small baby. She remarked that it was not as bad as she had feared it would be. David's needs seemed to be put first during the first two months in that Michael's feeds would be constantly interrupted by David needing something. Michael seemed not to object and it made me wonder whether he was naturally placid or if he had already learned that he would have to wait. David was included wherever possible and Julie did not panic when he went near the baby. He touched the baby's face but it often became a poke or a slap. Julie stopped him then.

There was very little eye contact between Julie and Michael while feeding as she was often responding to David or keeping a check on what he was doing. Michael showed very little facial expression and rarely smiled. However, there was little individual stimulation during my observations. He spent quite long periods of time in a bouncing cradle inside a large play pen. Michael appeared to be content to sit and stare at the lights and more recently began to examine his hands which had been enclosed in mittens for eight weeks or so because he might scratch his face.

There had been a noticeable difference in the handling and stimulation of Michael over the last few weeks. He was admitted to hospital with feeding problems and a heart murmur had been detected. Julie began making more eye contact with him and played with him and talked to him after a feed. I was relieved to see there was beginning to be some response.

David was very active, very verbal and interested in his surroundings. He clearly let people know if there was something he needed or wanted.

I found this period of observation very stimulating, a good learning experience, exciting and at times very painful. I found it difficult to comprehend that a child of David's age could perceive the changes that were going on in his family. There were definite stages of development which were worked through with the help of his parents. It seemed as if David knew that his mum had changed physically and emotionally by the way he was able to adapt without extreme distress. The efforts to help David become more independent were worked at by both of them. David knew it was important for him to respond and he did. Since Michael's birth he continued to try to do things himself but sometimes asked for my assistance when he knew Julie would ask him to try again.

David's constant search for something was also very evident at times. I felt he connected me with bringing it. After Michael's birth he looked quite perplexed when I arrived until he had examined my handbag. It was as if I might produce another baby.

Julie worked very hard to make the arrival of the baby as painless as possible for David. He was well prepared for a child of his age and continued to develop well. It has been an excellent experience for me and has already been useful in my work. I look forward to teaching observation in the future.

Part V
Getting into deep waters

11 Kerrie: A view of an infant survivor   95

12 Sam and James: Can you hear me mother?   103

Introduction

Occasionally students may find their observation experiences presenting problems, the complexity of which could not have been fully anticipated. While sustaining child observation as the primary purpose for meetings, observations may be fulfilling strong and essential functions for other people in the household.

Kerrie's observer, following her through a succession of placements, inevitably became the only person who knew of Kerrie's different carers and increasingly played a vital role in supporting Steve as he tried to parent Kerrie unsupported and in poverty. The essay conveys different levels of involvement and in particular the skills required to sustain the primary task of child observation.

Above all, the essay provides a unique and disturbing account of the distressing experience of a young child in the care system.

The author of the essay about Sam and James could not have anticipated her learning about the impact on behaviour of child-minding in a family. As with the account of Kerrie's life in care, the learning from this observation is relevant for practitioners and a very unusual although painful dimension in considering the nature of day-care provision. Although presenting a disturbing account of James' experience, the author reminds the reader of the distortions inevitable in the observation process: "The need to tidy things up, make it simple, can undermine our understanding". Child-minding, therefore, needs to be considered from many dimensions in order to reach balanced conclusions about a child's total experience.

11 Kerrie: A view of an infant survivor

This observation arose from an interest in the experiences and adjustments of children who move between caretaking situations. When seeking a child I mentioned interest in a child moving to adoption. I have seen the child just 41 times, employing the principle as far as possible of not instigating action but following the child's lead throughout an intended year-long observation.

Kerrie was found through negotiations with a local authority social services department. She had at this stage been in care for one month following admission on a place of safety order.

Throughout the year of my study the child experienced split care. Mother left her at 15 months and a care order was made at 19 months. Father actively considered adoption during Kerrie's twenty-second month, but her return home was agreed without warning one week before her second birthday.

The parents

Kerrie is the only child of Ann and Steve. As boyfriend and girlfriend aged 18 they were mutually involved in surviving unemployment and enjoying night clubbing and substance abuse to relieve the boredom. Ann's pregnancy was unplanned. Steve declined marriage but attended the birth, which was quick and uncomplicated. The family lived in Steve's father's house. Ann moved out at Steve's instigation because she was unwilling to care for the house or the baby; Steve assumed care of Kerrie for three weeks. In the fourth week Ann obtained custody of her daughter and resumed caring for her. One week later Steve received a year's custodial sentence for burglary. Ann, for the same offence, was given a six-month sentence. The prison service allowed Steve to visit Anne and Kerrie throughout their detention.

On release, mum and Kerrie lived in a flat. The period up to reception into care accounts for about 10 weeks. The application for a place of safety order followed a phone call from one of Ann's aunts stating that three days earlier Kerrie had been left with her. The aunt said that this could no longer be tolerated by the family. Ann has shown no interest in Kerrie since her departure in Kerrie's fifteenth month.

On release Steve lived in his father's home. After one month he sought contact with Kerrie.

If you find the above summary difficult to follow then your reaction parallels exactly that of being an observer of Kerrie. Engagement has taken me into five households. I have had direct contact with 15 adults and 22 children. Traditional methods of gathering information by asking questions, would under these circumstances have been very superficial but maybe would have cushioned me. This observation gave me an acute sense of the child's perspective. My 40 hours with her felt like one of life's longest journeys. It was easy in spite of my observer role to feel responsible as within two months of involvement I became the only adult in her life who had followed through all the changes. Kerrie's story is set in a small city in the north of England. Without exception her carers were working class.

At my first visit Kerrie was 13 months and two weeks:

A large golden haired little girl, she sat on the settee in her mother's small living room staring straight at me. Showily dressed in pink and white frills I had a real sense of mum being glad of an opportunity to display her attractive daughter to someone. After checking that I was nothing to do with Social Services and that I would play no part in assessing her as a carer, mum lifted her daughter off the settee onto the floor as if to signal that the observing could begin.

Kerrie was offered various toys including a ball which she stretched out to reach. Mother then thought of further questions to ask and I was distracted from the child for probably two or three minutes. My attention returns to her as mum begins to look in her direction. Kerrie has pulled herself up to balance against a coffee table in the corner.

She advances towards an ornamental frog. Mum firmly says "no", the child looks at her, then advances again and touches the table, but not the real source of her interest.

I wondered in retrospect whether this denoted a child who had learnt to deny her own need to explore and experiment in the interests of keeping mum content.

Confusion threatened this first encounter when mum using a colloquial term "Will you watch her then?", asked me to babysit while she went to the shop. The speed of the request left me flummoxed. Did she believe the social worker to have introduced a free babysitter?

The child looked at me as I sat opposite her and then she looked at mum's slippers. I rolled the ball and she concentrated on trying to return it. After some minutes she looked around as though searching again. She looked at me but continued the game before I even realized that mum had returned. The little girl was on her feet advancing towards the door.

Having observed this stoicism when left with an absolute stranger, I was relieved to then view the following intimacy between mother and child:

Mum puts down the comb and scoops Kerrie up. Placing each of the child's feet under her armpit, she takes each of Kerrie's hands and gently swings her. She carries Kerrie back up into the room and as she swings Kerrie head down towards the floor chants, "Kerrie's falling, Kerrie's falling". The little girl giggles and yells excitedly. This is repeated six or seven times until, laughing loudly, the two fall exhausted onto the sofa.

The totality of Kerrie's trust in her mother was striking. As I left shortly after this exchange, I was unaware that I would never observe in mum's house again.

The next two weeks I called at mother's home unsuccessfully. The third week I visited the foster home. This is already Kerrie's second placement. The first broke down prior to my initial contact after just 10 days when a small birth child of the household had bitten and smacked Kerrie. This second placement is within walking distance of birth mother's house in order to facilitate daily contact. (The previous placement at a double bus ride distance had resulted in just two visits in 10 days.)

Kerrie in foster care

Foster mother describes Kerrie as taking first steps, using a few words, chattering more and with encouragement imitating clapping and singing. I see Kerrie moving around and mouthing much more, but apparently less solidly contented and appealing, prepared for the day with less individual care:

Foster mum says mum had not shown up for Kerrie for six days. Kerrie is playing with Jane, a younger child, on the floor. Jane started tugging at the toy Kerrie was holding. Kerrie whimpered and struggled, she looked around as though to see if foster mother was looking and then "aiyee" relinquished the toy to Jane. A little later Kerrie became quite distressed; probably teeth I was informed. Comforted with a bottle, the little girl is placed in her pram. A burst of the cuckoo waltz, the household's very distinctive doorbell, sounds. Foster mother enters the room in advance of Ann who sits down, says hello but doesn't move towards her daughter. Foster mother lifts the child out of the pram onto mother's knee. Ann holds the child loosely and explains her health and financial difficulties. No questions about her daughter's wellbeing. Kerrie drops her bottle on the floor, mother automatically picks it up repeatedly and then suddenly says "No Kerrie, no". Child laughs, then threatens tears. She is still watching mum's face. I get up to leave feeling disappointed for the child that mum was so in need of attention as to divert attention from her.

I had seen Kerrie subsuming her needs first to those of the other younger foster child and then to her own mother. Additionally, this little girl was physically unwell. This latter feature was to recur frequently.

Within days of this visit the foster family went on a week's holiday leaving Kerrie with other foster carers. I was asked not to visit (what message mother got I do not know). Three weeks later:

As I rang the doorbell I again noted its distinctive sound. Kerrie was under a table in the corner, my efforts to greet her and establish eye contact were rejected. Birth mother has not now visited for 20 days and Kerrie is described as difficult, clinging, no longer speaking or chewing food. The doorbell rings, Kerrie comes out from under the table and stands looking to the door. An aunt comments it's about the fifth time and clearly every time she hopes it's her mum. How physically altered she looks. Her cheek pads have shrunk, her eyes are dull and cloudy, her movements lack fluidity, her gait is wobbly and unsure, surrounded by people she looks very apart and makes very soft whimpering noises. Some display by Jane is being applauded by the adults. Kerrie picks up Jane's bottle; "No" says foster father. Kerrie says "aiyee, aiyee" and totters to the extreme end of the room. She places herself under the highchair and picking up a 10-year-old's training shoe proceeds to hit herself around the head with it.

Shortly afterwards I leave overwhelmed by Kerrie's despair. The adults' apparent myopia seemed to be their way of coping with the impossibility of getting alongside the child's grief. Three days later Kerrie's social worker rang me to say the child was transferring to another foster home.

Visit to fourth foster home

Ten days later Kerrie has been described as settling well. Foster mother attributes this to a lack of competition (the next oldest child in the house is nine years). I witness a pleasant hour playing and pottering. The evident healing that had occurred had left the child physically and emotionally stronger and therefore able once more to explore, imitate and rage. Nevertheless I experienced her wellbeing as fragile, as shown by poor frustration tolerance:

Foster mother Sally advances and extracts the work box from behind the chair and places it high on a cupboard top. Kerrie rages, pushes the toys on the floor to one side and grabs from me a part of her sorting toy that I had abstractedly picked up. When Sally entered the room Kerrie moved nearer to her. Kerrie played with sorting cups on the floor, changing the TV channel several times, watching tigers in a documentary on the TV, played with my key ring and registered verbal annoyance with my incorrect assembling of her sorting toy.

Subsequent visits to the foster home enabled me to observe Kerrie's developing relationships with its eight inhabitants. She grows in her skills and tolerance; my view is extended considerably and intimacy develops between us:

She set off down the path. I followed her explorations. She looked up at a passing cabbage white and I had a real sense of someone having encouraged Kerrie to watch such. Some humming from across the hedge seems to attract her. She went still and listened. I picked her up and we saw flowers, a cat and a figure bending, gardening.

I completed this write-up mindful of Alessandra Piontelli's observation (1986): "helping to keep interpretative impulses at bay so that the language naturally remains unburdened by jargon but rather tends towards the poetic".

I noticed after this visit that Kerrie is chewing, chatting, climbing and growing. The only remaining recognition of her loss appears to lie in foster mother's observation that "in the event of any two members of the household getting physically close, Kerrie invariably attempts to insinuate herself between them".

Quite suddenly, without my knowledge or any prior warning, the birth father informed Social Services of his wish to care for his daughter. Suspicion stalked in Social Service's earliest comments about him, but within weeks of family introductions commencing, I was told Kerrie would now spend each daytime in his care.

I accordingly negotiated permission to observe at father's residence and for the first time had the opportunity to observe her motivation to bond being mirrored by the primary carer's commitment. My apprehension that dad too might be a source of hurt through broken attachment was quickly allayed, although, for the period of our contact, never completely.

I liked dad at my first visit and found Kerrie demonstrating loving:

Once in the back area of the garden Steve said to Kerrie: "Let's find the bambi". At this point I noticed both rockery areas were liberally dotted with dwarf and animal figures. Kerrie approached one of these, lent slightly into the flower bed and, placing both arms on it, gently kissed a bambi figure. This action was repeated in respect of several of the more accessible figures a number of times. Kerrie was picked up by dad to stretch across and love a couple of dwarves sitting at either end of a seesaw.

Later when dad is in the kitchen making tea as we sit together under the awning of a swinging garden seat, she pulls a blue strip of plastic out of her mouth and gives it to me. She stands on the seat of the chair, puts her arms around my neck and very gently kisses me.

Before I leave I observe dad getting her to sit in a high chair. She shouts, bangs, kicks and cannot believe it when the food disappears into the fridge to cool. When the curry arrives she eats quickly and for the first time in my knowing her she uses a knife and fork.

As her daily pattern is established, Kerrie apparently adjusts. Collection by dad at 8.45a.m., return to bath and bed at foster home at 6p.m. In many of my visits I am ignored, frowned at and admonished for a wrong-doing. Dad asks if being so rough, hitting so much and "all these NO words" are usual for little girls of 18 months. He worries when she hits other children in the park. He repeatedly shows immense patience with her interest in all items that are forbidden and is not surprised when the foster household's kitten quite badly scratches her in response to tail pulling.

Late August dad goes on a planned holiday:

On my arrival Kerrie is asleep. In talking to foster mother I learn that Social Services are concerned regarding dad's plan to live independently of his father. The phone rings. I go to Kerrie while foster mother chats to her caller. I say hello, she looks at me frowns and then puts her head on one shoulder. When foster mother tries to distract her she kicks. When lifted down onto the floor Kerrie stumbles and cries inconsolably. Foster mother notices Kerrie pulling at her ear and queries an ear infection. She goes off to the phone to arrange a doctor's appointment.

I am told the next day that foster mother's diagnosis was correct and with a couple of doses of antibiotic she was seemingly less troubled. I ponder Kerrie's extreme physical reaction as a metaphor for her rage. Having watched it gradually build as her confidence in the bonds with dad developed, it was as if it roared out in response to his disappearance.

Kerrie in her father's care

On September 6 Social Services were awarded a care order. Steve was irked but not antagonistic to this provision but he did have expectations that his daughter would within a week or two be allowed to reside in his care.

Having withstood the delay of court proceedings it was now announced that Kerrie should stay by night in foster care until such time as her dad settled in his own house.

By November dad's intolerance of the uncertainty of waiting is so pronounced as to be affecting the care he offers. My record of 12 November notes a grubby house, a child with a dirty dress and a lack of toys available for play. The following week I arrive to find Kerrie unwell and seeking attention. As the hour progresses she examines every item individually in my bag. It evokes an intimacy which suggests forfeiture in other relationships.

In the course of my visits it becomes more and more difficult to focus on the child rather than her immediate parent. I talk of feeling stuck when I share recordings with my seminar group. As depression hits the household I get drawn into it and fail to recognize my own need to avoid the painful truth that the parenting is just not good enough for the prognosis to be positive.

Following the awaited house move Kerrie once more spends large amounts of time in her foster mother's company and appears to flourish. Her negative expletives and frowns greet me less often. She adds to her vocabulary and looks generally healthier. Christmas does not provide the expected landmark of her return to nights at home. Foster mother is irritated as the need to manage her own sense of loss at the envisaged parting is an ever pressing issue. Dad becomes anxious, depressed and ambivalent; he talks of going on holiday to Africa, of getting full time work and seeking adoption for Kerrie.

January

I visit late one afternoon. As I enter dad barely looks up. Kerrie looks dishevelled and is mouthing a sorting toy:

> *"I'm bored", says dad, not taking his eyes from the TV. "I'm not sure I can go on with this much longer. This fellah I know thinks he can get me a job."*

Kerrie is responsive when I initiate some play with her but she lacks concentration.

I wonder if this is a reaction to dad's mood:

> *"It all keeps going round and round in my head; I phoned Jean and she said she must come and talk to me about adoption."*

Before I leave I experience a pang when I see Kerrie's tea, a cold sausage roll and a bag of crisps served on a paper bag on a foot stool in a house warmed by just one element of a gas fire.

At my next visit Kerrie has a cold, but whether this reflects her usual attunement to loss of attention or is the obvious result of the twice daily journey in the pushchair it is hard to tell.

And then one day dad just doesn't turn up to collect her, the only unplanned absence in seven and a half months. I am glad I have an incomplete grasp of what Kerrie made of that day. On a planned visit to the house I found dad sitting in semi-darkness too ashamed to face the world, despairing as a result of having run out of money for food. I agree to accompany him to the foster home the following day.

Kerrie is among the boys, generally rummaging around. I am struck by how much better she looks than on my last visit, when she was quite messy and fractious.

On re-entering the room she picks up the disintegrating telephone directory. Dad doesn't move; no object appears to hold her interest; she picks up a crayon and quickly scribbles on the chair cushion of an armchair. Dad remains engrossed in his phone call. The door opens; foster mother walks in, "Mum" says Kerrie holding the crayon up to show her.

Dad indicates his need to talk to her. She sits down and he tells her about his difficulties. I hear the kettle boil. I get up and go to make the coffee. Kerrie follows me into the kitchen and asks me to pick her up. I do so and explain for some minutes what I am doing. The breakfast room door is opened, suggesting a change of tempo in the conversation.

I am putting used cups into the filled sink and as the door opens saying "slosh". This seems to dispel Kerrie's pensiveness. She is happy to be placed back onto the floor and obligingly responds to my request that she open the door. Kerrie is very pleased with the completion of the door opening. She repeats it several times, laughing loudly. Her enjoyment appears prompted by sensing a change of adult mood.

I found this visit very difficult. There were clear expressions of anxiety in Kerrie, the obvious way she lingers at my side while the tension between her two principal carers is expressed. Also I saw with clarity the immature father too personally depressed and self-absorbed to be capable of responding to his youngster. For the remainder of my visit to the house Kerrie was energetic and entertaining; saying a number of words; singing and seeking sociable games like tickling and hand rhymes.

As I presented this visit to my seminar group, I became troubled and angry realizing eventually that Kerrie's development had been on hold or depressed for all but two weeks of the preceding three months. Once again I realized this little girl had been communicating her anxiety and loss through a physical mechanism. The weeks following the sharing of anxieties between dad and foster mum witness an upturn in the interaction between father and child. I see new physical skills and hear many new words. The wait is still there, but somehow it is less forlorn. During the visit at the end of the first week in February Kerrie says "biscuit me peas" and by herself takes her nappy off and uses her potty. Four days later, without apparent explanation, Kerrie's return home was agreed.

Return home; "Coming to terms"

So finally father and child are observed adapting to one another alone at last from the panoply that had peopled my view of the first 11 months. Potty use and emptying is achieved within three weeks. Phrases begin to pour forth "down, toys, play", "pennies in my box", "not yours, mine, Dad's", "pull again, me do it". Gross motor skills now include jumping from stairs, walking up unaided, carrying items like liquids in containers straight, jumping into the swimming pool.

Dad is moving around gathering up items for Kerrie's evening out at the foster mother's. As she models my shoe, he turns and gives her a parental look of approval, the like of which I have only seen from him once before. This provokes me to comment that he does seem more settled in himself. He agrees that he is, "money still does my head in but I've decided not to worry about it". The three of us leave the house. As we go through the gate Kerrie reaches up for dad's hand and stands still at the kerb edge. As we are driving in the direction of the foster carer's house, dad says that he had taken Kerrie to visit on Saturday and that with the four recently-arrived under 10s, the place had been "too much". Kerrie had "brayed the baby", she was jealous. "It was difficult for her, so we went to the baths."

101

Dad has difficulty locating the house and three times gets out of the car to approach houses. Kerrie remaining seated comments and points in dad's direction. I see her as unperturbed even when he disappears. Eventually the correct house is found. Inside Kerrie hangs on to dad's trouser leg. He picks her up. I leave in an attempt to make "goodbyes" easier. After a few minutes dad appears. In the short journey to his destination he tells me that Kerrie hadn't cried. The younger children had gone and got some dolls and started playing with her.

As I wrote up this early March visit I had a strong sense of no longer needing to hang onto a spirit of hope for this child. Finally, in just under one year she has acquired a psychological parent, someone with whom she can be secure in the knowledge that she is of value.

12 Sam and James: Can you hear me mother?

Choosing a focus for this paper from so rich a variety of experiences has been the most frustrating part of the course. The choice was eventually provoked by trying to explain to a social work practice teacher how the observation process can contribute to our ability to attend to the communication of others.

Even where people share a common culture and language, listening to others and making sense of communications demands considerable effort and skill. Emotional obstacles to hearing and receiving create even more powerful barriers. George Eliot saw that "If we had a keen vision and feeling of all ordinary human life, it would be like hearing the grass grow and the squirrel's heart beat, and we should die of that roar which lies on the other side of silence". To protect ourselves from being overwhelmed she suggested that "the quickest of us walk about well wadded with stupidity" (Eliot 1871). Over a hundred years later Menzies Lyth (1988) described the way that a hospital profession institutionalizes practices which can prevent nurses from "coming effectively into contact with the totality of any one patient". Social work has its own protective mechanisms.

The opportunity to concentrate on interaction between a child and his parents over an extended period has enabled me to see how selective tuning in and out of communication can be an organized, systematic process reflecting family myths and functioning.

The child I observed, Sam, was 18 months old. His parents, Janet and Sean, are in their mid thirties and play an equal part in looking after Sam. Janet used to go out to work and Sean works in a hospital; both are professional people. Sam is their only child. There are two children, James and Gemma, who are minded part-time and most of my observations took place when James was with the family. James is a month younger than Sam but taller and more heavily built. His mother is called Pat and his father, Tony. They work together in a printing business and participate jointly in his care at home. Gemma, nine months, lives with her mother, a single parent and is minded in the afternoons when her mum goes to college.

The following observations give some flavour of the family's childrearing values and the way Sam is being brought up:

Sam sits down to play with his circus train. He picks up a giraffe and says something to Janet pointing to the giraffe's neck. Janet confirms that giraffes have long necks. Sam pushes the train around and Janet suggests Sam gets his chair and makes a tunnel. Sam fetches the chair and pushes the train between the baby walker and chair but cannot get it past the chair leg. He says 'uh uh' to Janet. She tries to advise him how to fix it but then gets down on the floor to help.

Sean comes in with a book and Sam climbs up onto the sofa, settling himself comfortably close to Sean who puts his arm round Sam and gives him a squeeze. Sam pays close attention to the book pointing at the pictures and saying 'de dee' to most things

103

though he can say 'Pooh' (for Pooh Bear) and something that might be 'Piglet'. Sean reads the story, pointing out some of the things in the picture and asking Sam to point out others.

Sam is quite confident about gaining positive responses from others and free in his approaches to them. Sometimes his behaviour has an experimental feel. What will happen if I do this? The following two pieces are from the beginning and end of my observations.

Sam fetched a book from the shelf and brought it to me with a smile. He put it on my lap and began to turn the pages saying, or rather commanding, me to read as if he were used to having adults do as he wished.

As Janet and I were sorting out dates, Sam crouched down behind me. I felt his hand on my foot. He was trying to lift it up like a blacksmith shoeing a horse. He looked carefully at the heel of my shoe, running his hand over it, exploring it. He put my foot back and repeated the process with the other foot.

I felt as if the observer was being observed, and after this we felt more comfortable with each other. In this family, physical contact seemed to be a means to resolve all kinds of problem situations as many of the examples from the observations show. Janet, in particular, seemed to have an overriding belief in the efficacy of 'kiss and make up'.

I think I only saw Sam express uncertainty on one occasion. He had misread Sean's action and thought he had done something wrong. Perhaps his reaction was intended to diffuse any potential anger his parents might be feeling towards him as a result of a misdeed he did not understand.

Sam leaned towards Sean who extended his arm so that the coffee mug he was holding was as far away from Sam as possible. Sam screwed up his face as if genuinely distressed and about to burst into really upset crying (Sam can be quite theatrical). Sean reassured Sam, saying, "the coffee is hot". Sam's face unpuckered a bit but he looked for assurance to Janet by puckering up his face again. She came over and said he needed a proper hug and a kiss and put her arms around him kissing and reassuring him.

Janet and Sean seemed to have a clear set of values and ideas about good parenting and the child they wished to raise. Janet appeared to work particularly hard to live up to her ideal of a good parent, which seemed to involve constant activity with the children and never showing negative feelings. All the physical and emotional effort put into Sam's upbringing seemed like a heavy burden Janet could not acknowledge even through the half-serious remarks parents often make about parenting and their children. However, she did frequently complain of being tired and worn out. Initially I wondered whether Janet's close involvement with the children, the constant round of sand and water play, books and puzzles may have been stimulated by my presence as an observer. However, as I spent more time with the family and the patterns persisted, it seemed rather that Janet needed to convince herself that she was a good parent.

From a distance Janet's efforts seemed heroic. However, I came to feel as oppressed, as I think Sam may have been, by her attempts to direct and shape him. Almost all the observations contained some example, short or extended, of Sam needing to defend himself from intrusions and the direction of his play. As Sam evidently expected that those around him would take notice however, I felt confident that he would succeed in getting his message across.

I was struck by Sam's ways of coping with the intrusions of the adult world. He has a large repertoire as the following extracts show:

Sam was playing with his Duplo train. He says what sounds like 'more' pointing to the empty carriages. Janet helped him find more people and he put them into the train. Janet then suggested he fix some bricks to the carriages and fitted some on for him. He pushed her hands away, pulled the bricks off and continued to arrange the Duplo people. Janet brought the engine and began to undo the train to couple up the engine. Again Sam pushed her hands away and put the train back as it was.

Sean and Sam have been playing with some small Playpeople and furniture for about 10 minutes. Sean has been making suggestions, helping to fit things together and asking questions, like "How many desks are there?". Sam says "three" (which, if the table is included, is right). Sean says "no, not three. How many desks?". Sam says "two desks". They go on arranging the schoolroom pieces and Sam puts the people by the chairs. He then carefully turns all the chairs, tables and desks upside down. Sean begins to straighten them up but Sam puts them upside down again and Sean then understands that this was what Sam wanted.

Sometimes Sam had to work harder to get himself heard given Janet's difficulties about acknowledging angry feelings.

Janet suggests that they play with a farm set. Sam fetches the box and empties the pieces on the sofa. Janet says he should put the pieces on the floor. Sam is reluctant and eventually throws them on the floor in an angry, challenging way. Janet sits on the floor trying to coax Sam to arrange the animals. She gives him instructions: "Find the hen and her chickens". Sam points at the pieces but withholds his attention and doesn't really co-operate. Janet persists. James has got back into the peddle car. Sam sees this and goes over and pushes James out. Sam gets into the car and moves it to the centre of the room. Janet ignores this and goes on giving instructions about the farm animals. Sam responds half-heartedly, not wanting to get out of the car and risk James moving in. Janet is clearly getting edgy, since Sam won't do what she asks, but does not confront him and eventually sets the farm animals out. She tells me that now Sam will knock them over. Sam drives the car to the edge of the farmyard and stops. He says 'stuck' and pushes the car angrily backwards and forwards a few times though he could easily have driven the car through the animals had he minded to do so. Janet says he must put the game away. Sam protests and begins to whinge, sitting in the car whining "moo, moo; and honk" and pulling at his penis. (Sam has just begun to use a potty and can manage more easily without his pants.) Although she is angry Janet seems uncertain about whether to have a direct confrontation or to deflect the anger. In the end she mimics Sam's whine and they both begin to laugh.

James provides Sam with a safe substitute on which to vent his angry feelings. James can be relied upon not to retaliate and Sam rarely suffers real reproach for behaviour towards James. Although there were many occasions on which Sam appeared to be quite deliberately winding his mother up, she never openly expressed the anger which she clearly felt. Sometimes Sam's provocation seemed to play on his mother's dislike of overt expressions of anger and aggression.

Sam began jumping on the chairs and sofa. Janet told him that this was not allowed but it only seemed to spur him on. He seemed determined to provoke some sort of showdown. He jumped vigorously on the sofa between his mother and me hitting out at Janet and catching her face. He then hit my face. Janet caught both his hands and hesitated as if wondering what she should do. She was plainly angry but biting it back. Perhaps she wanted to yell at him or even hit him back. She threatened to put him out of the room, then tried to divert him by telling him to tell and show me things. This had no effect and Sam went on struggling with Janet and I felt she was struggling with herself. In the end Janet began to tickle Sam. Sam threw himself about enjoying it greatly and it all ended with much kissing and cuddling.

It seemed as if this family tended to avoid the expression of negative feelings and I found myself wondering about Janet's experiences in her own family. Her restraint felt more like a self discipline born of conviction than something with its roots in the past. I felt Sam must be wondering what he would have to do to make his parents mad at him.

Sam seemed both to understand and be able to challenge the way placatory gestures operated in the family but I wondered what he would make of them in the long-term and how it would affect his development.

Janet told Sam that he was standing on a toy puppy and to 'give it a love'. Sam hesitated as if indicating that he is not going to do as suggested. Then he picked up the puppy and rubbed it against his cheek. He went over to Janet's chair and banged the puppy down hard on the wooden arm of Janet's chair catching Janet's hand several times apparently quite deliberately. Janet made no comment either about her hand or the assault on the puppy which had previously required 'a love'. She evidently chose not to respond to Sam's challenge.

Sam could still express his own negative feelings but I wondered how far adult anger might remain a worrying mystery for Sam.

Sean suggested that the boys might like a story. Sam purposely picked out Jack and the Beanstalk, gave the book to Sean and said 'read'. Sean said 'You don't like this story' but Sam said 'read'. Sam settled himself on Sean's lap ... Janet said to me in a stage whisper that Sam got upset with the giant. Sean read and Sam concentrated hard ... Sean got to the bit where the giant chases Jack down the beanstalk when Sam suddenly took the book and snapped it shut. He appeared not to be distressed, but decidedly wished to know no more. Sean said 'You don't like the giant, do you' and Sam said 'No' in quite a matter of fact sort of way.

In one of the observations described above, Sam uses James as a safety valve to discharge his aggression. My observations in Sam's family, the reports of colleagues in the seminar group whose observations also included minded children and my frequent contact with another family with a pairing very like Sam and James suggest that minded children may be used by families in very similar ways.

The contrast between Sam and James could hardly have been greater. James was pale and often blotchy faced, sad and slow, usually on the edge of things, while Sam pranced centre stage bright eyed and bushy tailed filling all available space. One of the most painful images of the observations is of James standing frozen and wretched in the middle of the living room with a piece of banana seemingly stuck to his hand. He seemed powerless either to eat it or to put it down.

Apart from being a safety valve for Sam's aggression, James was someone that Sam could manage and control in the way Janet seemed to control Sam.

James was happy to have the peddle car back. From time to time Sam went over to 'help' by turning the car round or getting it on the grass, neither of which James wanted. James clearly resented this interference and began to cry each time it happened. No one took any notice.

James and Gemma and the other minded children, seemed to play a vital role in supporting Janet's role as the "good mother". Janet frequently referred to James' problems and slower development as a way of emphasizing Sam's achievements and positive qualities. At times she seemed to find it difficult to let Sean play his part. Nine months old Gemma, unlike James, is seen as a bright and happy baby.

Sean is walking round with Gemma on his hip. They are cooing and smiling at each other and obviously enjoying one another's company. Janet comes in from the garden where the boys are busy with the peddle car and tractor. Janet says Gemma needs a cuddle and takes her from Sean. Gemma begins to wail and protest. Janet tries to soothe her to no avail. Janet sends Sean off to collect the shopping.

But it is James' communication and behaviour that is most persistently distorted. It is apparently accepted by all concerned that James is having such a good time that he is unwilling to go home. Here are two pieces, one from the earlier observations and one from the end which suggest otherwise.

Janet opens the door to let me in. Sam is close by her. James is standing at the bottom of the stairs, looks at me, his face crumples up and he begins to cry bitterly.

The children are playing in the garden when I arrive. Sam is in the peddle car. James looks up, takes half a step, sees that it is me and then looks away, his shoulders drooping.

My time for observation was towards the end of the afternoon when James would be expecting his mother or father to collect him. James' behaviour when I arrive clearly shows disappointed expectations. Over the 10 months he has learned to contain his feelings but they are still quite evident if anyone were prepared to tune into them.

That James does still look forward to his people coming for him attests to the strength of need children have for their own parents. One might otherwise see his anticipation as an example of the 'triumph of hope over experience'. These examples are fairly typical of what happens when James' parents do arrive for him:

James' father arrives to collect him. James becomes animated for a few minutes and runs to his father to be picked up. Tony picks him up without a word, not even looking at him, and continues to talk to Janet over James' shoulder about Pat and James' hospital appointment.

Pat arrived to collect James. James ran to her whimpering. She picked him up but paid no attention to him and went on talking to Janet.

On each of these occasions and on most other occasions when I observed James' departure, James did indeed end up crying and protesting about having his coat on, getting into the buggy or the car, and was often still crying as he and his family went down the road. These signals were read by both Janet and James' parents as indicators that he was having such a good time with Janet that he did not want to go home. James tries to make himself 'heard' the best way he can – by yelling and screaming. The trouble is that when James does fuss, cry or even scream with rage at going home time, his behaviour is interpreted to fit the needs of the adults. Not even the acquisition of language helps James get his feelings and wishes understood. Here is a recent observation:

Sam, James and Janet were in the back garden washing the big toys. Pat had arrived early and was talking to Janet. James was concentrating on washing the seat of the tractor in a mechanical, abstracted sort of way as if it were merely something to fill in time. Pat decided she had to go and ask James if he wanted to come too. Before James could reply, Janet said that James did not want to go, so Pat left. James asked where she had gone and said 'Want home'. This was ignored ... James returned to his abstracted washing of the tractor seat, trying to look a part of things. Pat returned and praised both boys for their work. James watched her covertly. Janet said she did not think James would want to leave. Pat tried to cajole James - unnecessarily, as he was in fact standing waiting patiently, showing no signs of resistance. James did then begin to struggle and resist Pat's efforts to get him into the buggy and ready for off. Pat was not being drawn in and took what seemed an inordinate time getting James strapped in. James by this time had worked himself up into a full scale temper tantrum. Neither of the mothers spoke to James. Janet talked sympathetically to Pat, commenting that James never wanted to go home.

This interpretation of events seemed to underline Janet's role as the good caretaker. For James' parents perhaps it was an example of Eliot's 'wadding of stupidity'. Was it simply too difficult, or guilt provoking to see that being minded was not a happy experience for James? James' response was reminiscent of those recorded on film by the Robertsons in their studies of young children separated from and then reunited with parents.

It would have been easy to conclude that James would be crushed by these experiences, but there were indications that James too, like Sam, could find ways of managing his own needs:

Sean was sitting on the floor, legs stretched out. Sam gave Sean the book he had chosen and settled himself on Sean's lap. Sean offered to make room for James. Sam said, 'James read' in an inviting sort of way. James chose to remain on the floor but settled himself close against Sean's legs. While Sean read the book Sam had brought, James 'read' his own book. Sean kept an eye on James ensuring that he got his books the right way up.

James seemed content to choose a degree of closeness and involvement that suited him and his choice was accepted. In the next example, James seemed to be using a joke to get his mother's attention:

Pat came for James. While Janet was talking to Pat, Sam was pushing at his mother's bottom (he had been angry with her). Janet ignored Sam but James noticed what was going on and went over to his mother smacking her behind, saying 'Bottom'.

This paper has been about communication, though the observations have highlighted a number of themes which warrant further exploration. The most important theme has been the question of minded children. In addition to coping with being away from their own parents and familiar settings, such children seem vulnerable to playing a part in the dynamics of the minding family. The anxieties that parents may have about leaving their children seem likely to reduce the ability to see or hear their child's experience and messages.

One of the most difficult aspects of the observation has been to watch how James' communication in particular has been either denied, ignored or shaped to belief systems necessary to sustain the adults' view of the world. However, the observer does not remain a neutral party to the process. I had come to feel quite angry and frustrated with both mothers for what seemed their wilful deafness to what both children seemed to be trying to say. However, re-reading my observation notes, I see that in my construction of relationships, I too had edited things out. Sam was much cherished and loved. His confidence indicated that he did expect to be understood and have his needs met. There were many times in which James' misery was noticed by Janet and cuddles and consolation were offered to him. The need to protect ourselves so well understood by George Eliot may not be the only enemy to our willingness to listen to others. The need to tidy things up, make it simple, keep it straightforward, can also undermine our understanding and ability to hear what we are being told.

Part VI
Application of learning from observations for social workers, practice teachers and tutors

13 George: Transferred learning from child observation   113
   to social work and practice teaching

Introduction

Throughout this book, authors have made reference to their personal and professional learning. Through observing George, the author paid attention to the relevance of what she was seeing to her professional practice as a social worker and as a practice teacher and presented her thinking and conclusions in her essay.

"CCETSW requires that students' practice must be directly observed in relation to the six core competences. Direct observation of practice must take place a minimum of three times in each assessed practice experience." (Extract from *Assuring Quality in the Diploma in Social Work-1: Rules and Requirements for the DipSW* CCETSW 1995, para 4.4.1). ""The evidence for the practice assessor's report will be derived from the candidate acting as a practice teacher on a minimum of two occasions" (*Assuring Quality for Practice Teaching* CCETSW 1996, para 5.5.2).

The author of this essay is able to demonstrate the relevance of observing George to her own professional development, thereby indicating the potential for others.

13 George: Transferred learning from child observation to social work and practice teaching

This essay describes how the Young Child Observation Course enabled me to re-evaluate the way in which I practise. I will be looking at the development of my ability to think about some of the theoretical concepts I used and their usefulness for social workers. I will then look at how the course helped me in my practice teaching. I will begin by looking at the initial experience of observing myself in my relationship with the child I observed and the learning that came from this.

I observed George aged two years who lives with his mother Carol, his father Alan and younger brother Tim, aged six months. They were a white family living in an owner-occupied Victorian house in a multiracial area of South London. The mother cares for her two sons at home; the father works outside the home.

The first piece of major learning came for me in my struggle to define the role of observer and withdraw from my usual role of social worker. I needed aims and objectives; and very clear ones. I felt lost without a clear definition of what exactly I was expected to do. My fear of going into an environment without these was overwhelming. I work in a team of colleagues and workers proud of its clarity about the social work role and experiencing constant frustration about the lack of clarity in multi-disciplinary team work in the hospital. We have also managed to stave off cuts in our establishment by using our clarity. I would imagine this is not an unusual experience in social work. There was also my own personal investment in goal-focused work. I feel much safer if I am clear about the purpose of my contact.

I learned that it was this very struggle to define the observer role that was a goal in itself, that the process of just staying with the discomfort was one of the learning experiences. The absence of a pre-defined role helped me to understand how its presence could prevent me from seeing and paying attention to what was in front of me and how that develops over time. I was learning "not to try and understand everything at once but to give a kind of unbiased attention to every point that arises and to await further developments". (Briggs 1992, page 49) This was not comfortable for me. I was grateful to the lecture and seminar groups which referred to the "turbulence" that results from such endeavours helping me to feel less isolated. This course helped me think again about "process" in relation to my work.

I learned from having the opportunity to observe, to place myself in a situation where I had an essentially passive and self-defined role. I experienced a strong pull towards wanting to become involved in an active way. I was enabled to stand back from my normal way of working, to slow down and examine in detail the relationship I had with the child. The observations helped me to observe my own ways of reacting and patterns in my relationships.

One of the patterns I struggled with was my powerful need to be helpful. Martha Harris (1987, page 233) writes about observers wanting to justify their presence by doing something to help. In my first observation session I wrote:

The lump of 'playdoh' is in a plastic bag. He asks his mum to get it out of the bag. She encourages him to do this. He tries to; she tells him to get it out. I end up turning the bag upside down ... (In other words I get it out of the bag).

In one observation (the ninth) the mother actually stops me from being over helpful:

George keeps throwing his button-type things on the floor and I pick them up ... Carol says that I will not pick them up any more unless George says "please" and then I will only pick them up once more.

The latter example also highlights the dilemmas that can arise from being reactively "helpful". I was trying to give George what he wanted, which I thought were the objects on the floor, but which became the fun of throwing them and having me pick them up. I was also trying to tidy up for his mother. I felt trapped in this process. This reminds me of how I sometimes find myself trapped by wanting to be helpful at work, and how I need an external voice (my manager) to help me out of this pattern with clients, other professionals or students.

I also became aware of how much more comfortable it was to have a proactive role, in this example to teach George something so that he would do things in the "correct" way. In my fourth observation I write about play with a Russian doll:

We play with this – pulling it apart and putting bits together (I have a strong pull to wanting to put it together 'properly' – he just mixes all the halves up). George plays a kind of hide and seek with the various parts of the doll and wraps them up with a bit of netting.

Another example, at my sixth observation, was when I was observing Carol help George make a picture:

She (mother) gave him a bit of glue, pictures from the Guardian newspaper of people, ... paper, milk bottle tops and glitter – in a shaker. She then left him to it. He glued the picture folded up and put glue on both sides of it. She dealt with this by sticking it (the paper) round the corner. (I am continually impressed by her tolerant flexibility with him – her lack of 'shoulds' and 'should nots'!). He glued things on top of each other. She gave him dried lentils and pasta. He enjoyed dropping them from a great height and showering everything and missing the glue ... (I felt a very strong pressure to organize him, stop him putting everything on top of each other – make the picture "pretty").

I clearly remember the conscious effort I needed to make, to stand back and observe or participate as passively as I could. I write in observation number eight:

I have to adjust to being so passive and find it quite uncomfortable and feel quite powerless trying to observe.

I also remember the relief when I occasionally had what I thought to be a good excuse to be directive, proactive and do something "properly". For example, in my twentieth observation:

Somehow, I don't remember how, I got onto making a car-type thing out of the tinkertoy (plastic shapes that fit together including wheels and long straws) – this was great fun for me but George was not that interested.

The need to do something was so strong that when it came to writing it up I don't remember how I got into doing it. I am left wondering how much I do things almost unintentionally in my work. I am also sure that in this example there was a strong wish to play with a toy which was really interesting to me.

The observations of George faced me with choices about how active or passive I could be and how involved or close to George I wanted to be. Unlike observing a physically dependent baby, George was mobile, active, sociable and loved telling me what to do. I had the option of either following his play responsively, or standing back and observing him playing and refusing to get involved, or pro-actively directing and leading the play. The third option was what I would have done as a social worker. Prior to starting the observations, I would have regarded the second option as the most neutral and educational. However I found myself doing the first option most of the time.

This allowed me to reconsider the whole question of "psychological distance" (Mattinson 1975, page 24) between worker and client. As a social worker I am not only working with the outer world but also the inner experience of the outer world. I have to have skills in balancing an awareness of people's inner experience of the world with the outer reality. This is particularly so in my work with people who have experienced the death of their baby. If I was not able to share these peoples' grief and distress I would not be able to counsel them. However, if I did not attain some distance, I would not be able to assess how it is I can be most helpful. I would become overwhelmed by their experience of loss.

Shopenhauer's story of the porcupines (Mattinson 1975, page 24 quoting Freud) helped me to think about this:

"A company of porcupines crowded themselves together one cold winter's day so as to profit by one another's warmth and so save themselves from being frozen to death. But soon they felt one another's quills, which induced them to separate again. And now, when the need for warmth brought them nearer together again, the second evil arose once more. So that they were driven backwards and forwards from one trouble to the other, until they discovered a mean distance at which they could most tolerably exist."

What I found most useful is the idea that we have to experiment to find the most tolerable distance. There is not a "correct distance". Nor, as Mattinson also points out, can the worker "always be the arbiter of this distance". The psychological distance between George and me changed according to how he was, how I felt and how involved his mother wanted to be. I now realize that I assumed that I should be able to control this distance and that it should always be the same both with George and with the people I work with.

Mattinson (1975) refers to Menzies Lyth's work (page 27) in looking at organizational defences. This leads me to think about the ways in which the team of which I am a part, develops rules about our distance from clients, the work we are prepared to do and the type and clarity of referrals we are prepared to accept. I wonder if this is partly about our need to keep a "sufficient" distance from some very distressing situations and distressed people. However, I am also interested that we all regularly break our own rules. Maybe this is actually quite healthy and we can always resort back to our quills/rules when we start to feel the other's quills/distress too keenly.

Two other aspects of my learning were related to the process of reflection, and the significance of a conflict of views between myself and the seminar group.

I presented my ninth observation to the seminar group and found myself feeling distressed, not heard, angry and confused by what the group were saying to me. I felt that I was in a double bind. They were questioning how positively the mother of George presented - maybe I was not seeing all there was to see? Maybe George's mother was masking depression and not presenting a true picture of herself? I felt disbelieved and undermined. I gradually realized that I felt trapped; that I could not win. If Carol continued to present in the way that she did, my observation skills would be questioned; if Carol did not, and presented some shadow then the group was proved right and I had not seen what was in front of my eyes.

I missed the following week's group due to an urgent and unforeseen work commitment, though I have to acknowledge it was with some relief as I still felt angry, confused and unheard. At my next observation of George he was very obviously angry with me. It started to click. Was I reflecting his feelings to me back to the group? In which case I felt I had to reflect them back to him. I write:

George was hitting me with a wooden spoon, it hurt as he was doing it quite hard. I said that hurts me. He looks at me as if he does not know whether he wants to hurt me or not. I said "you don't know whether you want to hurt me or not". He stopped hitting me.

I stopped feeling hurt and angry with the seminar group straight after this visit.

Thinking about my anger towards the group, I remember that one of the issues that I had wanted to discuss when I presented my ninth observation was my confusion about my role. I write at the end of the ninth observation:

I feel a bit lost in conflicting demands and expectations. ... At the beginning of each time I go, I feel quite "roleless" somehow and (I find) that's anxiety-provoking.

This had, unusually for the group, been ignored. I wondered if I had actually picked up some confusion and anger from George? Maybe this was about George not really knowing why I visited him and what he could expect from me. Maybe he was unheard. At the end of the ninth observation George tells me he likes my hair, and asks if I will be having supper. I tell him I am not. George only says "bye" after encouragement from Carol. Here was George expressing positive feelings towards me and asking what would I be doing and not getting a clear answer back. Maybe he thought I was not staying for supper because I did not like him, but I kept coming back to see him and I played with him and I guess he knew I liked him by the way I was when I was with him. So who was this woman who stayed for an hour, had a coffee, whom his mother liked and who would not stay for supper?

We discussed it in the next seminar group and agreed that some process of reflection seemed to have happened. Maybe George was uncertain about my relationship with him? We decided it was important for me to talk to George again about the reason for my visits.

During my twelfth observation I tell him about the course and about how I come to see him to learn about children. After I say this he is very creative in his play, he seems to want to appreciate me and be appreciated. He is very clear about what he wants me to do (be under the table with him, his toy cars and his plastic road map) and he gives me a present (cars wrapped in road map) and asks me to give him a present in return. He is very appreciative of my present. He is also able to voice openly his feelings about me going:

I then say ... "I have to go very soon". He ... tells me to play cars. I say "no, I have to go to work now". He says "no". I say: "I'll be back next week". He says "coffee". I tell him "I've had my coffee and it's time to go". He does not look happy.

This open resistance to finishing continues to the end of my observations, which I think indicates that he now understood why I was there and was able to voice some feelings about that.

This experience was extremely useful for my learning in a number of ways. Firstly, it confirmed for me the usefulness of the concept of counter transference. Mattinson (1975, p.45) writes about this type of counter transference:

When the client attempts to make the worker feel what it was like to be him(sic) ... and when this is reflected in the supervision, the worker is telling the supervisor what he (sic) had to endure in the interview.

I think that I felt George's anger, hurt, powerlessness and uncertainty, without being aware of this and experienced it in relation to the seminar group. I think George was uncertain about my relationship with him. However, I also think that he may have been feeling very uncomfortable about his powerfully ambivalent feelings towards his younger brother. In the eleventh observation visit prior to him hitting me, he hit Tim. During the twelfth observation session:

She (Carol) expresses a lot of concern about George hurting Tim. She has dreams that she comes downstairs and finds Tim has been murdered by George ... She then tells me how on some days she just screams at him – sits on the settee and shouts.

Maybe I accepted his projection of unbearable mixed feelings towards his brother. He may have felt that he was not being heard by his mother, and in fact could not win in the relationship to her as she was so angry with him. The seminar group then reflected this back to me. Is it possible that my acknowledgement of George's ambivalence – not knowing whether to hit me or not – (in Carol's presence) enabled Carol to acknowledge her ambivalence towards George the following week?

The other lesson for me was the importance of being heard in supervision. I trusted the group enough to be able to say that I did not feel heard by them. This enabled me to explore the process that had gone on and stop acting out the countertransference. I know that when I am being supervised and my point of view is being dismissed, I often give up my view, believing that I have got caught in something and cannot see straight. Mattinson (1975) writes:

... I am not happy when these phenomena are taken to be just the weakness of the worker with a complementary denial of the strengths of the psychopathology of many social work clients. If the workers are led, even very subtly, to feel ashamed of their interaction and ability to withstand some of its grosser manifestations, their professional growth will be inhibited ... supervisors do not have to be above their own reactions, but can value them as 'highly informative reflections of the relationship between client and worker', giving them a clearer realization than any words could do of the pressure the client is exerting on the worker ...(p.47)

In fact I would go further and argue that an understanding of the process of reflection is essential to the supervision of social work if unacknowledged feelings and sometimes abusive dynamics are not reinforced. Loughlin (1992) writes about a supervisory group:

"Case after case highlighted the fact that the worker was unconsciously mirroring the situation of the abused child within the family and was subjected to the projections of colleagues, managers and the wider network ..." (page 113).

I now want to relate my learning on this course to my practice teaching.

First, I realized how frustrated I can become watching somebody else learn at their own pace and in their own way, and how tempted I am to do something for them. When I observed George I was able to see how my interventions could prematurely interrupt the process of his exploration, enjoyment and learning. I learnt to tolerate the feelings of frustration which arise when I do not follow my impulse to intervene and teach. Conversely, I realized how rewarding it can be to follow the process and reflect back to him what he was doing.

For example in my first observation, early on in the hour George is playing with a toy and wants me to do something. He asks me to do it a number of times and I always say "you do it". I was thinking that he should do it for his own learning and that my role as observer meant being as physically passive as possible. His mother remarked on how I was "not co-operating". I remember feeling like a professional adult in this particular piece of interaction. Later on in the same observation visit I try a different approach encouraged by his mother's remark about my lack of co-operation:

He gets the workbench toy and hammers screws and bolts and says "you hammer" to me. I hammer and say "you hammer" to him. This carries on with George becoming more directive – which one he wants me to hammer and which end of the hammer to use.

I now feel more attentive, open and in tune with the process of his play. I am also relieved of the responsibility to encourage him to learn and can enjoy seeing how he does things and how he wants me to do things.

Observing George, writing the observations up and attending the seminars, led me to think about the process of learning for my student. I realized that she did not learn by example – in fact she just copied and then forgot. However, she was able to learn by being encouraged to think about her work and she was able to use feedback from my observations of her. She had to be allowed to make her own way and then encouraged to review and think about what had happened.

I realized that the most productive way of supervising my student was to reflect back to her what she was saying to me and encourage her to think about and learn to evaluate and question her own work. She began the placement thinking and feeling that she had no learning needs. She ended it, by telling me that she would always carry in her head my encouragement to her to think about what was happening in her work.

Briggs (1992, page 50) writes about the importance of separating the processes of observation and theorizing. This facilitates "the development of the ability to see, hear, feel and to understand" and "with the avoidance of premature 'knowing'". In my relationship with George the structure of the course undercut my tendency to be overly proactive and responsible for the process of the relationship. I carried this learning over into my relationship with my student.

I learned to be available to receive the projections of another, to pay attention to these communications and to follow "the lead given by the other (...), in a receptive, attentive and observant way "(Briggs 1992, page 50). This learning enabled me "to see, hear, feel and to understand" the dynamics that were being played out in my relationship with the student I supervised. She, I realized, experienced the world as persecutory and herself as helpless in the face of overwhelming odds and a victim of circumstances beyond her control. I was able to use my realization about her experience of the world to prevent myself becoming overly caught in these dynamics. The course has enabled me to develop a "capacity to remain in doubt or uncertainty long enough to understand rather than to reach prematurely for fact or certainty".

The development of observation skills in my practice teaching gave me a way of assessing students based on the reality of how they actually practised, rather than on assumptions based on how they were in supervision or in the team.

The course enabled me to develop skills in observing my student practice, note down what I observed, and share with her my assessment of her skills and strengths, and where I felt she needed to reconsider or change. I was able to develop a style of practice teaching based more on observation and less on assumption. As I was more open about the basis for my assessment, my student could more easily challenge me and was less likely to experience the assessment as being out of her control. I think that it is extremely important to develop ways of practising in as open a way as possible as a practice teacher, partly for the reason given above, but also because it provides a model for how, I hope, the student will practise with her clients.

I was able to see how useful it was to have a way of challenging my student which did not feel destructive. I had previously had feedback, from a student I had supervised, that I could afford to be more challenging and less supportive. I had actually assumed that I was far too critical. It was extremely valuable for me to witness how this year my student did not fall apart from the weight of my feedback. In fact, she valued it and learnt from it. I think that the way in which we reflected on the observations in the seminars provided me with a safe enough experience of receiving and giving feedback, which I internalized and used in my practice teaching.

I have also been led to think about my supervision of students in the light of Mattinson's writing about the use of transference and countertransference in supervision and my experience in the seminar group. Mattinson (1975, page 127) puts forward a convincing argument for the supervisor to work "more on the interactive content of the interview and primarily with the countertransference, trusting the student's intelligence" rather than with the transference in which the supervisor works with the student's motives, assumptions and history.

Following the presentation of my ninth observation I felt helpless in the face of the group's view, and then later, immensely relieved and re-skilled when I talked about my feelings and realized that the dynamics of countertransference and reflection may have been at work. For me it was more enabling than to look at the transference and it confirms for me the importance of carefully unpicking the dynamics of the work in supervision and the benefits of using these concepts.

To conclude, the course has given me another perspective on my practice as a social worker and practice teacher. It has enabled me to learn about a way of using psychoanalytic concepts and the process of observation to practice in a more thoughtful, considered and process-oriented way.

Postscript: Some Ways Forward

Different aspects of the authors' learning are explicit in these essays. Implicit in all of them also is the wealth of potential learning for child care professionals.

Since 1994 CCETSW has funded annual recall days for tutors and practice teachers involved in the training. Those attending have taken the opportunity to reflect and share ideas arising from their experiences of establishing their own child observation training courses.

The nineties have proved to be a favourable time for innovation in response to both the requirements of the Children Act 1989 and to the changes in social work training at DipSW and PQ levels. By 1995 many child observation courses had been established in DipSW programmes and to a lesser extent in social services departments.

As confidence in the value of child observation as a rich source of learning has been established, the debate has shifted towards how best to provide this experience taking into account agency resources. College tutors at recall days have reported being able to arrange for children to be observed within their placement settings, thus both easing the problem of finding a child and enriching partnerships between tutors and practice teachers.

As the training has evolved, the many students observing young children in day care settings rather than in the child's own home has been striking. The restrictions on allocation of local authority day nursery places to children in need (Children Act 1989) have also affected the range of children observed. Inevitably there have been repercussions when students have confronted some of the issues of institutional care, so poignantly described by Jenny's observer, and by children with special needs and disabling conditions. The need for strong support and careful guidance cannot be underestimated.

Child observation experiences for DipSW students have been short-term, usually involving about 10 weekly one-hour sessions. Setting up these courses and facilitating learning has involved tutors in detailed preparation and planning. The manual on child observation, to be published as a companion to this volume, is therefore, a welcome addition to literature available to trainers especially where students are at the beginning of professional training.

For the many other professionals employed by local authorities to care for other people's children, observation training offers immense opportunities. A way forward being piloted by one training department involves multi-disciplinary groups of child care staff. Foster carers, child minders, residential staff, and playgroup workers benefit both professionally and personally from sharing, through the medium of observation, the stresses of doing very difficult jobs.

There is potential for extending this training to professionals in health and education, in the spirit of enthusiasm for multi-disciplinary working expressed in the Children Act, Part III.

These essays therefore provide a foundation for further developments. They are neither definitive nor prescriptive. Instead they provide insights into a dynamic process of learning which has the potential to help professionals to provide children and their families with the sensitive services they need and deserve.

The article printed on pages 123–132 is reprinted from the *Journal of Social Work Practice* Volume 5 No 1, 1991 pp.51–60, with the kind permission of the authors and publisher Carfax Publishing Company, PO Box 25, Abingdon, Oxon, OX14 3UE.

Appendix

The contribution of observation training to professional development in social work

JUDITH TROWELL* & GILLIAN MILES**

Tavistock Clinic, London

Summary *This paper first describes a range of uses of observational training and the learning to which it can give rise. It goes on to describe in detail a specific project that was undertaken by the authors with a selected group of social work trainers. The range of observations undertaken by the participants is described and their own comments provide first-hand evaluations of the experience. Observation is seen by the authors as one of the most important foundation skills in social work practice. They conclude by sketching out the possible place of such training in the social work career continuum in the UK.*

Introduction

> Throughout the three years of social work with the Beckfords, Ms Walstrom totally misconceived her role as the fieldworker enforcing care orders in respect of two very young children at risk. Her gaze focused on Beverly Lorrington and Morris Beckford; she averted her eyes from the children to be aware of them only as and when they were with their parents, hardly even to observe their development, and never to communicate with Jasmine on her own.
>
> (L. Blom Cooper, London Borough of Brent, 1985.)

Why is it so difficult to see what is going on in front of our eyes? In 1953 James and Joyce Robertson made the film 'A Two Year Old Goes to Hospital' and, rather like the conversion of St Paul on the road to Damascus, we were all forced to see what really happens to a child during hospital admission. The Robertsons were not the first to be aware, but because of the power of their presentation on film, the painful effects of hospitalization could not be avoided. Spitz in 1945 described the destructive effects of long-term group care on infants, and Winnicott in 1941 described what is seen if babies are observed, but both of these accounts were written material that could be overlooked. The Robertsons in their series of films forced awareness of the child's world onto the consciousness of professionals and the public. Others have looked at vulnerable groups in the population: for example, Irving Goffman (1958/61) in *Asylums*, focuses on mental patients. It seems that the only way in the first instance that anyone can see is by combining a determined and courageous stand, with a research passion to find out.

In the early fifties the use of infant observation as a training tool began for those intending to work with troubled and disturbed children using a psychodynamic approach. A child analyst,

---

Correspondence: *Consultant Child Psychiatrist, and **Senior Clinical Lecturer in Social Work, Child and Family Department, Tavistock Clinic, 120 Belsize Lane, London NW3.

Esther Bick, introduced the practice of systematic observation of the development of infants. This consisted of the student observing a baby, starting as soon after the birth as possible, and observing once a week for an hour over a year. Notes were not taken at the time, but students were expected to record in detail afterwards the interaction that they had observed, the emphasis being on what had been seen and felt rather than the students' own explanations or speculations on what might have been happening. This written account was brought for presentation to a small weekly seminar of three to six people where each student presented their material at least twice a term in the presence of a seminar leader. The task of the seminar was

> . . . to explore, on the basis of the available evidence, the emotional events between infant and mother and the other members of the family present during observations. There may also be a babyminder or nanny sharing in the care of the baby and this might be part of what is directly observed. The aim is to describe the development of the relationships between infants and others, including the observer, and to try to understand the unconscious aspects of behaviour and patterns of communication. Over time, a picture emerges which embraces a good deal of knowledge of the characteristic dynamics of family interaction. Aspects of the inner world of the family members which underline their personalities and relationships become manifest. In particular, the creation of the infant's personality, the interaction between constitutional and temperamental factors in the baby and the particular strengths and weaknesses of the holding environment can be considered.
>
> [Margaret Rustin (in Miller *et al.*, 1989, pp. 7–8)].

An early explanation of the method can be found in a paper by Bick (1964). From Mrs Bick's start within the child psychoanalytic field the use of infant observation spread geographically and spread also in terms of its use. Young child observation developed out of infant observation, firstly by extension for child psychotherapists of their observations, then other professional trainings such as those for doctors, nurses, teachers found young child observation a useful training tool. Family observation has since developed, but is more difficult to manage. Institutional observation has proved easier and highly productive, and students have observed in a range of settings, such as supermarkets, offices, shops, hairdressers, schools, day nurseries and hospitals. The research study by Bain and Barnett (1980), and the work of Menzies Lyth (1988) describe examples of institutional observation in practice. A significant lead on institutional observation has been offered by Obholzer and his colleagues at the Tavistock Clinic, although the work awaits formal publication.

In the 1980s there has, however, been a blossoming of accounts of infant and young child observations, including Stern (1985), Piontelli (1986), Waddell (1987), Brafman (1988), Miller *et al.* (1989).

The use of observation in social work training

The concept of observation is not new in social work training. Some social work training courses have required students to carry out some form of observation, usually of group care, and not necessarily focusing on any one individual subject over time. Some post-qualification social work courses, usually specifically in child care, have had observation as a component module. An evaluation of five of these courses carried out by the DES shows that some students felt that the child observation module had been central to their learning on the course and 'the most useful thing they had ever done' (DES, 1988).

Why has observation not developed in social work training, or lapsed where it had been used? This would seem to be for a number of reasons. First, finding a suitable subject to observe and setting up a contract can be very stressful. Then, students can become anxious because they are unclear about the observer role. The result of this is often that students appear to become bored. Again, the content can be very distressing and students who become upset may cease to attend.

The observation seminar depends on the skills of the seminar leader and, skillfully run, provides a setting where anxiety and distress can be safely discussed, thus enabling learning to take root at a deep level. The leader's knowledge from experience of the power and the usefulness of observation as a training experience is vital if the meaning of the task is to be sustained. All too easily observation can become a superficial, meaningless exercise.

What can social workers learn from observation? In their professional role they are required, bearing in mind issues of race and gender, to assess, monitor and make decisions and judgments about situations involving complex human relationships, which are often highly charged emotionally and where action may have far reaching consequences. We would suggest that, prior to any action, social workers need to be capable of taking an observational stance to give themselves the possibility of objectivity in coming to their conclusions. The observational stance requires them to be aware of the environment, the verbal and non-verbal interaction; to be aware of their own responses as a source of invaluable data, provided they are aware of what comes from them and what from their clients; and to develop the capacity to integrate these and give themselves time to think before arrivingg at a judgment or making a decision.

By the very nature of their task, social workers are constantly asked to work with acutely painful situations. As we will be describing, all the members of our course found aspects of their observations extremely painful; for example, to watch a child's needs being ignored or to follow the cumulative trauma of constantly disrupted placements for a small child. It is extremely difficult to bear such pain or the associated feelings that might be stirred by what is seen from the worker's own past experience. Action can so easily taken over as a way of avoiding the impact of what is seen, if it can be seen at all. Observation training, with its supporting seminars, gives the opportunity to reflect on the experience, and to understand and tolerate the emotional impact.

The mind of the trained observer needs to include several simultaneous functioning perspectives (see Fig. 1). In addition a range of other aspects of learning can follow from observing (Fig. 2). Observing can provide the student with an opportunity to become familiar

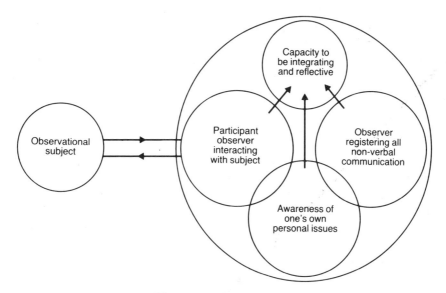

Fig. 1. *Mind of a trained observer*

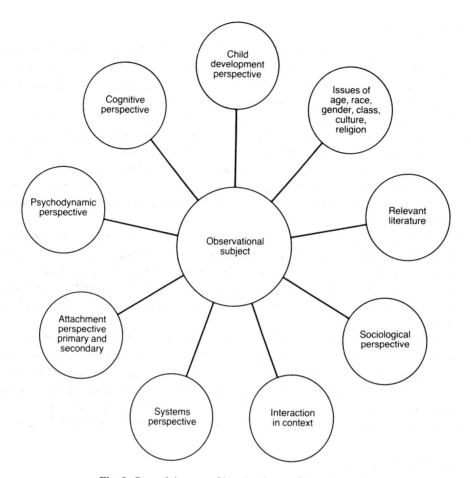

Fig. 2. *Some of the range of learning that can follow observation.*

with the individual's internal and external world (including issues of race, culture and gender), as a precursor to learning the skills of communication, e.g. a young child's observations lead to communication with other children.

We and our colleagues have used observation in social work training in the following ways in post-qualification courses.

1. *Child protection course.* Young child observation—10 weekly observations with 10 weekly seminars.
2. *Post-qualification child care course over 2 years.* Nine months weekly observation of an infant and 9 months weekly observation of a young child with weekly seminar for 2 academic years.
3. *Social work tutor's course to become observation seminar leaders.* Nine months weekly observation, mix of observations of infants and young children. Weekly seminar throughout.
4. *Multi-disciplinary group working with severely disturbed adults.* Nine months weekly observation of infant, with a weekly seminar.
5. *Course on organization and institutional process.* Two terms of weekly observation of an institution.
6. *Post-qualification specialist child care course.* Five fortnightly observations of young child with fortnightly seminar.

A specific project

The Report of the Inquiry into Child Abuse in Cleveland, 1987 (Butler-Sloss, 1988) was one in a long line of child abuse inquiries to point out the ease with which the child is lost sight of when there are very needy families and the difficulties, in these highly charged situations, of carrying out careful, thoughtful, thorough assessments.

The Central Council for Education and Training in Social Work, UK (CCETSW), in response to this concern about social work training, sponsored as one of its projects a Training in Observation for social work tutors who, it was hoped, would then become able to teach observation skills on their own courses. The hope was that over time this would create a growing number of teachers in the field. It was recognized from the start that the first priority was to train these seminar leaders and that the quality of the teaching obsesrvation skills would depend on the skill of the leaders.

Ten social work tutors from across the country joined this course for an academic year. They observed children ranging in age from newborn to 4 years, for 1 hour weekly. The children were a mix of boys and girls, cared for in their natural families, by a single parent, in care, in substitute families and in day nurseries. The children had a range of racial and cultural backgrounds; some were only children, some had older siblings and others had become the older sibling when a new baby arrived.

The participants attended a weekly seminar to consider their detailed recording of their observations. In addition, there were theory days to discuss various theoretical perspectives both on family relationships, child development and current research, race and gender, and on the application of observation to social work training. To conclude the training and to enable the participants to make sense of the experience, each member wrote a paper on an aspect of the observation, centred on a particular area of interest that had been sparked off for them.

Examples of some of the observations

Case history 1. A black child in an inner city day nursery 8.30–5.30, 5 days a week, where the first impression was of a bright, colourful, relaxed environment. What emerged was a picture of limited mechanistic play activities and the need to conform to such an extent that when a child, who for weeks remained silent, isolated, masturbating or sucking his thumb, joined in a nursery rhyme song he was told not to shout and to be quiet. The carers were, bar one, all white and their preoccupation was in gaining support from each other, e.g. at lunch time talking to each other, leaving the children to feed themselves, remaining unaware of the children's difficulties.

Case history 2. A child moved through five placements in the year. The number of adults and children in this child's experience became hard to remember, just as it was not easy for the observer to see the particular child because of the need repeatedly to establish a relationship with the adults and children in the new environment. When visible, the child's distress and withdrawal were painful, but only noticeable because of the comparisons possible over time, the child having been seen consistently in the different contexts. The child's resilience was impressive; when at last given permanence, her developmental progress was a delight.

Case history 3. A new baby in a middle class natural family aroused concern because of lack of responsiveness. Developmental delay was a real worry. Over time the mother's depression and exhaustion became apparent. The father was absent for long periods on business and the elder child repeatedly woke afraid at night. A few weeks after father's return the baby showed marked progress in development and seemed to come alive. Anxiety about developmental delay evaporated.

Case history 4. In a middle class suburb the central issue of the observation became whether this was a safe environment for a young child. The observer was constantly concerned as dangerous moments were perceived or recounted. The mother's state of mind was a worry, but there was always her accompanying explanation that what took place fitted with her own or her husband's cultural background (between the two all eventualities could be 'normalized').

The impact of the observation was powerful and unexpected to them. Finding a subject to observe was more difficult than they expected and this seemed to be linked to the problem of shedding their professional roles and feelings of vulnerability in a student role. It was not easy to find a comfortable way of being because the situation of observer was an untried role which was neither a professional nor a social relationship. They all became aware of the painful position of dependent small children, and the inadequate and inappropriate provision for them, and also aware of how powerless and hopeless the adults could feel. Most striking, however, was the ease with which they became concerned for the adults and on occasion lost sight of the child.

Examples of particular problems

In Case history 1 a black observer struggling with issues of racism and deprivation.

In Case history 2 the recognition by the observer that she had become the most consistent figure in the child's life, who at times seemed to know more about the child than anyone else. She felt the pain of knowing what impact the constant moves made on the child and the lack of support for a single teenage father.

In Case history 3 the overwhelming boredom of the observer only made sense when the depression and exhaustion of the mother were ameliorated and the unresponsive blob of a baby became a human being.

In Case history 4 the anxiety for the observer and the seminar group was invasive. Setting limits and boundaries were seen to be a problem for the mother not only in relation to her children, but also in relation to the observer, whose home and mind were invaded by it. This was mirrored by the ease with which the observation took over and invaded the seminar.

In none of the observations were the observers untouched by raw personal issues brought to the surface by what they were seeing. Another issue was the extent to which any crossing of social contact lines between the observer and the observed inevitably led to difficulties.

Comments from the course members themselves on the observation

Finding the observer role

> At our introductory meeting the little boy took me to see his bedroom and pointed to a map of the world on the wall, indicating Great Britain, saying that was the island where he lived. He pointed to a dot on the Southern Hemisphere and wondered what it was—I suggested a tiny island with which he agreed and then said that all that blue was the sea. As I struggled hard to identify an observer role, especially with a child this age (three and a half years) from whom pro-social interactions were so important, we were both children with maps beyond our comprehension.

The emergence of personal issues

> As well as being an observer observing a family, I was provided with further opportunity in the seminars to reflect about the observation process, both about what was

recorded of what was seen and about the nature of the perceiver. The seminar experience heightened awareness of myself as a participant in the group, as an observer of a child and as an individual. Increased self-awareness is not always a comfortable process, but the group was a reasonably safe place to explore boundaries.

Parenting issues and child development

I have listed a number of the tactics used by the mother to shape her son's behaviour. I find this interesting as many of the requests to me for help from parents when I was a social worker focused on bringing up their children to behave 'acceptably' according to parents' standards. The repertoire of my suggestions to help parents become effective were less subtle, more generalized, less specific, creative or contextual, lacking in responsiveness to the nuances of the child's emotional needs than are evidenced by this mother's range of methods . . . it provides justification for the observation of children in their own families by social workers.

Issues for assessment

I am still uncertain about the reasons for the baby's slow development; was this a response to the mother's depression in the early months or simply his innate temperament? Insofar as his passivity was a response to her depression one could suggest that he became more active as the mother became less isolated and more able to express some of her frustrations with her husband. I am also uncertain how far the judgement of slow development was arrived at because of the middle class expectations of the parents and the observer. Thinking about possible applications to social work assessments, I am sure that an assessment cannot be made on the basis of one visit; my view of the baby in the sixth month was certainly skewed by my own anxiety and I also failed to take sufficient account of the child's recent illnesses. Finally, I have been depressed by the social isolation and the process of gender construction which I saw in this family; I feel this reflects the social position of women.

Staying with uncertainty, not rushing to make judgments

If I had met this woman as myself, with my own personality, tending to be controlling, we might well have clashed. If I had gone in as the social worker with an agenda I might well have missed an important dynamic, and provoked a different response. As an observer, I was under no pressure to do, and so I could watch and wait. That absolution from doing made the space to see the observed, as well as to become aware of my own traits and feelings. . . . It was the *dissonance* between what I wanted spontaneously to do but contained that was the key to my understanding.

The pain of observing

I had anticipated a struggle with home observation in terms of maintaining my role. I had thought a good deal about detachment, rather less about attachment and the echoes of my childhood experience, and very little about the experience of counter-transference. Frequently there are references in the observations to 'distractions', to very powerful unexpected feelings and even, though not often, to the desire to escape.

The difficulty in seeing the child

I can well appreciate why social workers, when working with much more demanding and needy mothers than this motther, are unable to withstand being taken over by the parents' needs. The easiest observations were those where she and the child operated as a unit because then I didn't need to split my attention; by focusing on Mum I was of necessity focusing on the child. In those cases where the parent/child dyad does not even function as a dyad, it could be impossible to see the child unless you consciously imposed that on the person (against probable resistance). Thus, the need to reinforce that awareness in social work training is crucial, and perhaps there could be no better way to experience it than to come to it through being an observer.

The place of observation skills training in social work training

The following outline refers to the different levels of the career continuum of social work in the UK.

Basic training (Diploma in Social Work)

We would argue that the capacity to observe is central to social work practice whatever the specialism. Before any judgments and decisions can be made, the worker, in assessing a situation, needs to be able to observe from a boundary position, not totally engulfed, but appropriately involved. However skilled and talented they are, students entering the social work profession usually need to learn this skill. This is at the core of social work and, therefore, should be considered as part of the core social work skills learnt early in the course.

In discussion with the social work tutors we became aware of the enormous pressures on the curriculum. Another alternative might, therefore, be to place the observation and the seminar within the remit of the practice placement. Wherever placed the module would enrich the teaching of both Human Growth and Development, and Practice Skills sequences, but centrally it is about learning to adopt the observer role.

However tightly packed the social work curriculum, this can only be taught in an absolute minimum of five observation sessions, if the professional is to have confidence and competence in the observer role. This means five hour long observations, weekly or fortnightly, with five seminars alongside, preferably in small groups so that each student can present a detailed recording twice. (For further details concerning setting up observations and the role of the seminar leader see CCETSW (1990) Diploma in Social Work guidelines and an unpublished CCETSW paper).

Where students have chosen to specialize in child care we would strongly urge that the observation module be extended to a minimum of ten observations and ten seminars and, if possible, the observation subject should be a child under 5 years. This module could be extended to other specialities, such as the elderly, the mentally ill and those with learning difficulties.

Post-qualification phase

For those who have not had an observation skills module as part of their basic training we would strongly urge local authority training departments to consider organizing one for their newly qualified workers. Hopefully, it should consist of a minimum of 10 observations with 10 supporting seminars. As we have suggested for basic training we would suggest that observing a young child (under 5 years) makes an excellent introduction to observation skills. Some social workers in the post-qualification phase should be encouraged to consider undertaking an observation course for an academic year. This would enable them not only to acquire an observational stance, but also to gain some of the other range of learning referred to in Fig. 2.

Advanced award in social work

Observational skills should definitely be a module in any advanced training. The subject should be specifically relevant to the speciality. Alongside the specific skills acquired it needs to be stated that professionals gain from this experience both in their professional development and in their job satisfaction.

For anyone wishing to specialize in child care or child protection we would see an observation module as essential, preferably for an academic year (Pietroni, 1991).

Multi-disciplinary training

From our experience of running observation seminars on a specialist course we have found the training was enriched for participants by a mix of professionals, e.g. social workers, teachers, nurses, psychologists, doctors. As far as we are aware, however, no systematic work in this area has yet taken place, although serious interest in it has been expressed.

Seminar leaders

As with other specialities where the teaching is dependent on the knowledge and skill of the lecturer, observation skills training depends crucially on the atmosphere of the seminar and the competence of the seminar leader (Pietroni, 1991). Training, consultation and supervision will be required until there are sufficient numbers of trained leaders to cover training needs. Social work courses and local authority training officers could be encouraged to employ members of their staff who have done a post-qualification or advanced award observation as seminar leaders with consultation. As more people undertake these courses, resources will increase. Members of other disciplines, predominantly from the mental health field, could also be used as seminar leaders; at the moment child observation is perhaps more widely taught in other professions, so there is a resource that could be used.

Conclusion

We return to the comments of the social work tutors who have done our observation course and who vividly convey the advantages and problems if observation skills are to be taught in a meaningful way.

> This account reflects both the privilege I feel at being part of this learning experience and also the privilege of the life experience of this child. The features of the seminar which feel privileged are the time, the size of the group and the style of the learning environment, each of which contrast markedly with the constraints of the educational framework in which initial social work training operates.

> All this leads back to my final task, which was to connect this experience to the consideration of observation in social work training. In many ways the effect of the course was a reaffirmation of what I knew already, the validity and crucial role of observation in social work . . . the social worker, due to the prescriptions of his/her very role, has to impose on situations. But imposition without observation is skewed at best, and damaging at worst.

Acknowledgement

The authors gratefully acknowledge the contribution of Elizabeth Oliver Bellasis to the teaching on this course.

References

BAIN, A. & BARNETT, L. (1980) Design of a Day Care System in a Nursery Setting for Children under 5. Final Report. Tavistock Institute of Human Relations, Doc. no. 2347.

BICK, E. (1964) Notes on infant observation in psychoanalytic training, *International Journal of Psychoanalysis*, 45, pp. 558–566.

BRAFMAN, A. (1988) Infant observation, *International Review of Psychoanalysis*, 15, pp. 45–61.

BRENT, LONDON BOROUGH OF (1985) *A Child in Trust. Report of an Inquiry into the case of Jasmine Beckford* (London, HMSO).

BUTLER-SLOSS, LORD JUSTICE, DBE (1988) *Report of the Inquiry into Child Abuse in Cleveland, 1987.* Cm. 412 (London, HMSO).

DES (1988) *Five post-qualification social work courses: a research study* (London, HMSO).

GOFFMAN, I. (1958) The characteristics of total institutions, in: *Symposium on Preventive Psychiatry*, reprinted (1961) *Asylums* (NY, Doubleday).

MENZIES LYTH, I. (1988) *Containing Anxiety in Institutions: Selected Essays* (London, Free Association Books).

MILLER, L.,, RUSTIN, M., RUSTIN, M. & SHUTTLEWORTH, J. (1989) *Closely Observed Infants* (London, Duckworth).

PIETRONI, M. (ed.) (1991) Right or Privilege: post-qualification training for social workers with special reference to child care (CCETSW) (In press).

PIONTELLI, A. (1986) *Backwards in Time* (London, Clunie Press).

ROBERTSON, J. & ROBERTSON, J. (1953) *A Two Year Old Goes to Hospital* (Ipswich, Concord Films Council—and later films).

SPITZ, R. A. (1945) *Hospitalisation: an inquiry into the genesis of psychiatric conditions in early childhood. Psychoanalytic Study of the Child*, Vol. 1 (NY, International Universities Press).

STERN, D. (1985) *The Interpersonal World of the Infant* (NY, Basic Books).

TROWELL, J. (1991) Use of observational skills in social work training, in: M. PIETRONI (ed.), Right or Privilege: post-qualification training for social workers with special reference to child care (CCETSW) (In press).

WADDELL, M. (1987) *Infantile Development, Kleinian and Post-Kleinian Theory and Infant Observation Practice*, Tavistock Clinic Paper 55 (London, Tavistock).

WINNICOTT, D. W. (1941) *The Observation of Infants in a Set Situation*, Collected papers (London, Tavistock), 1958.

References and further reading

References

AHMED, S., CHEETHAM, J. and SMALL, J. (1986) *Social Work with Black Children and their Families* London: Batsford

BAIN, A. and BARNETT, L. (1986) *Design of a Day Care System in a Nursery Setting for Children Under 5* Occasional Paper No. 8, Tavistock Institute of Human Relations

BASSA D. M. (1978) 'From the Traditional to the Modern: Social Observations on Changes in Indian Child Rearing and Parental Attitudes' in Anthony, E. J. and Chiland, J. C. (eds.) *The Child and his Family* New York: John Wiley

BENTZEN, W. (1985) *Seeing Young Children: A Guide to Observing and Recording Behaviour* New York: Delmer

BICK, E. (1963) *Notes on Infant Observation in Psycho-Analytic Training* A paper read to the British Psycho-Analytic Society, July

BION, W. (1984) *Learning from Experience: Second thoughts and other works* Karnac

BLOM-COOPER, L. *et al.* (1985) *A Child in Trust: The Report of the Panel of Enquiry into the circumstances surrounding the death of Jasmine Beckford* London Borough of Brent

BRAZELTON, B. and CRAMER, B. (1991) *The Earliest Relationship: Parents, Infants and the Drama of Early Development* Karnac Books

BRIGGS, S. (1992) 'Child Observation and Social Work Training' in *Journal of Social Work Practice* 6, pp. 49-61

DUNN, J. and KENDRICK, C. (1982) *Siblings: Love, Envy and Understanding* London: Grant McIntyre

ELIOT, G. (1871) *Middlemarch* Penguin edition 1965, page 226

ELLIS, L., LASSON, I. and SOLOMON, R. (1996 forthcoming) *Keeping Children in Mind: Training Manual and Video on Child Observation* CCETSW

HANMER, J. and STATHAM, C. (1988) *Women and Social Work: towards a women-centred practice* London: MacMillan

HARRIS, M. (1987) 'A Baby Observation—the Absent Object' and 'The contribution of mother-infant interaction and development to the equipment of a psychotherapist' in Bick, E. and Harris, M. *Collected Papers* Clunie Press

HENNESSY, M. *et al.* (1992) *Children and Day Care: Lessons from Research* Liverpool: Chapman

KAGAN, J. (1981) *The Second Year* Harvard Press

LAMBETH, London Borough of (1987) *Whose Child? The Report of the Public Inquiry into the Death of Tyra Henry*

LEWIS, M. (ed.) (1991) *Child and Adolescent Psychiatry: a Comprehensive Textbook* Williams and Watkins

LOUGHLIN, B. (1992) 'Supervision in the face of no cure: working on the boundary' in *Journal of Social Work Practice* vol. 6, pp.111-116

MATTINSON, J. (1975) *The Reflection Process in Casework Supervision* Tavistock

MENZIES LYTH, I. (1988) *Containing Anxiety in Institutions* Free Association Books

MILLER, L., RUSTIN, M., RUSTIN, M. and SHUTTLEWORTH, J. (eds) (1989) *Closely Observed Infants* Duckworth Press

PIETRONI, M. (ed.) (1991) *Right or Privilege: Post Qualifying Training with Special Reference to Child Care* CCETSW Study 10

PIONTELLI, A. (1986) *Backwards in Time* Clunie Press

STERN, D. N. (1985) *The Interpersonal World of the Infant* Basic Books: Tavistock Clinic (1992 onwards) Understanding your One-Year-Old, Two-Year-Old etc. series, Rosendale Press

TROWELL, J. (1991) 'Use of Observational Skills in Social Work Training' in Pietroni, M.(ed.) *Right or Privilege*, and (with Gillian Miles) 'The Place of an Introduction to Young Child Observation in Social Work Training' in *The Teaching of Child Care in the Diploma of Social Work* CCETSW (see below)

WINNICOTT, D. W. (1971) *Playing and Reality* London: Penguin Books

Further Reading

BICK, E. (1964) 'Notes on Infant Observation in Psychoanalytic Training' in *International Journal of Psychoanalysis* 45, pp.558-566

BOWLBY, J. (1979) *The Making and Breaking of Affectional Bonds* London: Tavistock Publications

BOWLBY, J. (1988) *A Secure Base: Clinical Applications of Attachment Theory* Routledge

BRIGGS, S. (1995) 'From Subjectivity towards Realism; Child Observation and Social Work' in Yelloly, M. and Henkel, M. (eds) *Learning and Teaching in Social Work* Jessica Kingsley

CCETSW (1991) *The Teaching of Child Care in the Diploma in Social Work: Guidance Notes for Programme Planners* (Improving Social Work Education and Training No. 6)

FRAIBERG, S. (1959) *The Magic Years* New York: Scribners

GOFFMAN, I. (1961) *Asylums* Anchor

HARRIS, M. (1987) *Thinking about Infants and Young Children* Clunie Press

HOXTER, S. (1988) 'Play and Communication' in Boston, M. and Daws, D. (eds) *The Child Psychotherapist and the Problems of Young People* Karnac

MacKENZIE SMITH, S. (1992) 'A Psychoanalytic Observational Study of the Elderly' in *Free Associations* vol. 3, 3, page 27

McMAHON, L. and FARNFIELD, S. (1994) 'Infant and Child Observation as Preparation for Social Work Practice' in *Social Work Education* Vol. 13, No. 3

MITCHELL, J. (1986) *The Selected Melanie Klein* Penguin Books

MOSS, P. and MELHUISH, E. (1991) *Current Issues in Day Care for Young Children* Department of Health, Thomas Coram Research Unit, HMSO

National Children's Bureau Early Childhood Unit (1991) *Young Children in Group Day Care: Guidelines for Good Practice* NCB

Northern Curriculum Development Project (1992) *Improving Practice with Children and Families* (Antiracist Social Work Education No. 2) CCETSW

OAKLANDER, K. (1979) *Windows to our Children* USA Real People Press, second edition

PARKES, C. M. and STEVENSON-HIND, J.(eds) (1982) *The Place of Attachment in Human Behaviour* Tavistock

ROBERTSON, J. and ROBERTSON, J. (1953 onwards) *A Two-Year-Old goes to Hospital* and other films, Ipswich: Concord Films

RUTTER, M. (1991) *Maternal Deprivation Reassessed* Penguin

TANNER, K. and le RICHE, P. (1996) '"You see but you do not observe": the art of observation and its application to practice teaching' in *Issues in Social Work Education* Vol.15: 2

WILSON, K. (1992) 'The Place of Observation in Social Work Training' in *Journal of Social Work Practice* 6(1) Spring

WINNICOTT, D. W. (1978) *Through Paediatrics to Psychoanalysis and Other Works* Hogarth Press